Contemporary Lingerie Design

Katie Dominy

Contemporary Lingerie Design

Katie Dominy

LAURENCE KING PUBLISHING

LAURENCE KING

PUBLISHED IN 2010
BY LAURENCE KING PUBLISHING LTD
361–373 CITY ROAD
LONDON EC1V 1LR
TEL: +44 20 7841 6900
FAX: +44 20 7841 6910
E-MAIL: ENQUIRIES@LAURENCEKING.COM
WWW.LAURENCEKING.COM

A CATALOGUE RECORD FOR THIS BOOK IS
AVAILABLE FROM THE BRITISH LIBRARY.

ISBN 978 1 85669 650 0

DESIGNED BY CHARLOTTE HEAL
WWW.CHARLOTTEHEAL.COM

PRINTED IN CHINA

CONTENTS

INTRODUCTION ⤫

With the introduction of the word 'lingerie' during the mid-nineteenth century, underwear was transformed from being a purely functional item to becoming one imbued with overtones of seduction. Lingerie suggested everything from sultry temptress through to virginal doll. In the twenty-first century, the play of mixed references from different traditions and styles has turned these clichés into strong fashion statements in the skilful hands of today's lingerie designers.

Lingerie design is often regarded as a mystery, even by professionals working in other sectors of the fashion industry. Whereas ready-to-wear designers can showcase their work as it would be worn and will see women actually wearing their garments, lingerie designers have only their imagination and personal experience to draw on.

This difference comes across strongly in the advertising and photoshoots created by lingerie designers and brands. With designer ready-to-wear, visuals are aspirational but mostly set within the real world. Lingerie, by contrast, rather like the beauty industry, offers a fantasy world where lingerie-clad models appear in cornfields, city streets or nightclubs. To be a lingerie designer is to be able to create this imaginary world with a clear vision of the hopes and desires of the women you are designing for.

In this book, 30 contemporary lingerie designers explain how they work. They talk freely about what inspires them and the many unexpected influences that shape their choice of colour, silhouette and decoration. They have been chosen for their innovative approach to lingerie design, each providing us with a compelling insight into their working methods. Some have taken a straight path from fashion design school, whereas others have arrived at lingerie through a different route. But all are linked through their passion for the subject and the influences that surround it.

The history of lingerie is strongly weighted to Europe, especially France. This legacy continues today, with the largest percentage of designers included in this book coming from France. But the book also encompasses designers from around the world, and their cross-cultural backgrounds create a unique mixture of influences.

The history of lingerie is interlaced with the history of fashion. Up until the industrialization of Western Europe in the mid-nineteenth century, the two main components of lingerie – the corset and the soft lingerie of underwear, such as petticoats and camisoles – were not considered as separate items from clothing.

The traditions and techniques of the corset-maker evolved into the corsetry and bra industry we know today. The old corset-making techniques, which provide inspiration for many of the lingerie designers in this book, are under threat of vanishing completely from artisan production in Europe; the skills that took generations to refine are being lost as production concentrates on mass-production in Asia.

The soft lingerie, the frou-frou petticoats, camisoles and underwear, evolved from 'under-linen' and the wedding trousseaux of household and table linens and underwear items that were sewn in advance by unmarried girls. With nineteenth-century industrialization came mass-produced cottons, linens, laces and embroideries at more affordable prices, allowing these white lingerie pieces to become increasingly lavish and to reach a greater number of women. By the end of the nineteenth century, department stores had introduced ready-to-wear soft lingerie, which contributed to the decline of handmade trousseaux.

The artisan soft lingerie produced in Europe today is still strongly linked with home and bed linen, but, as with corsetry, production has shrunk to a few high-quality artisan companies. Yet, as with the corset, vintage crafted trousseau items are important influences for lingerie designers today.

Through the twentieth century, lingerie and corsetry evolved in tune with fashion, creating underwear to shape and enhance the ever-changing fashion silhouette. Lingerie was often the first apparel division to embrace innovative new fabrics, such as rayon, nylon and Lycra, as well as promoting the ongoing development of fabrics that offer support but are fine and light – the ultimate goal in lingerie.

In the 1990s, the explosion in designer fashion became the launch pad for many young lingerie designers. The growth in small luxury labels led many to choose lingerie as their creative outlet, being conscious of fashion, but also with a clear idea of their own 'lingerie world'. At the same time, many international designers extended their product line into other areas, which included lingerie alongside footwear, handbags and fragrances. In addition, the decade saw designer lingerie spring up not only in Europe and the US, but also in countries such as Japan and Australia and major cities in South America. This trend towards lingerie designers based outside of the traditional fashion capitals will evolve as fashion finds new hotspots and enthusiastic markets worldwide.

First and foremost, designer lingerie is a luxury item that evokes memories and fantasies. The desire to decorate one's body or someone else's in tiny wisps of silk, chiffon or lace lies at the heart of the development of lingerie and always has done. This book is an insight into how we do it today.

A.F. Vandevorst ❧

Behind the successful designer label A.F. Vandevorst is the Antwerp-based team of Filip Arickx and An Vandevorst. Their lingerie label Nightfall is designed from the same artistic and intellectual background, fusing elements of masculinity and femininity to form a new modern aesthetic.

Filip Arickx and An Vandevorst met (on the first day) while studying at the Fashion School of the Antwerp Royal Academy of Fine Arts — considered by many as a launch pad for the most experimental and inspiring designers of the late twentieth century. Around ten years after Martin Margiela and Dries van Noten graduated, An and Filip completed their studies in 1991.

After gaining experience in the fashion world — An at Dries van Noten and lecturing at Antwerp's Fashion School, and Filip as a freelance designer and stylist — the couple got married in 1998 and also started their label, A.F. Vandevorst, with a catwalk show during Paris Fashion Week.

'From our very first collection we included lingerie, as it was very important that we made a "total look" with shoes, lingerie, and so on. Under each outfit that we sent out on the catwalk, every woman was wearing our lingerie or garments like very feminine lingerie. Lingerie is the first layer that you put on in the morning and you build it up before you go outside. So this element is something intimate, delicate, very personal, and is also mysterious and secret. You don't know from the outside what people are wearing underneath and it's this play that we like to use sometimes in our garments.

'In the beginning, the lingerie collection was all made in Belgium, but then we were left without any manufacturers, so we had to stop making lingerie. Then in 2005, by coincidence or fate, we came into contact with a very good French lingerie manufacturer, so we picked it up again and decided to make a full collection. We are now supported by people who are very experienced in the technical side of making lingerie.

'We've started a negligée line that is more like luxury ready-to-wear then lingerie. It looks very much like lingerie but you can also wear it as daywear.'

THE THREE NIGHTFALL LINES
❧

'In the main line the mix of the two of us brings a certain duality to each garment. Because we are a man and a woman designing together, there is always a rough/strict side contrasting with a soft/feminine side — so it is a mix of both worlds. Nightfall also features this duality. We have one line called *Gender* where we play with contrasting masculine and feminine. This can translate itself into the material, like using cotton combined with lace, or in elements of men's underwear combined with very feminine elements.

'We have another line called *Infirmière*, ("nurse"), which features the red cross and the white and red of the logo.

'Our third line is called *Tradition* and there we play with the glamour lingerie of the 1930s to the 1950s, with corsets and really beautiful Hollywood-style lingerie.'

left to right:
Spring/Summer 2008; Spring/Summer 2008; Spring/Summer 2009

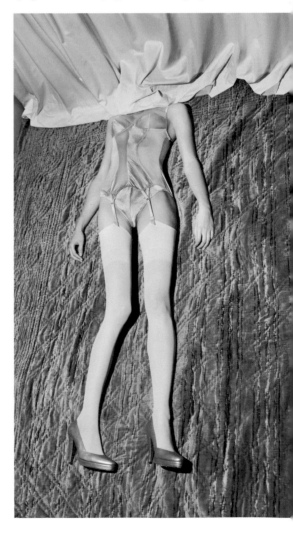

THE INSPIRATIONS FOR THE DESIGNS

F: 'When I first met An, we went to flea markets, where she was always buying things.'

A: 'I always bought old glamour lingerie that was really nicely made and had no stretch. Of course now you need the comfort of stretch; at that time it was very nice to have this shape but it was not comfortable to wear! But I always bought it. I liked the colours and often bought it only for the colours. I like the pink tones; it's soft, a kind of camouflage, fragile and delicate. I also have piles of old silk stockings; they're so beautifully made, they have such a nice texture and yet they're so fragile. It's amazing how much work there is in them. Inside them are all these ribbons, finishings and trimmings. They are like couture.'

THE NIGHTFALL AND MAIN COLLECTION

'The lingerie line is always started first. We begin by making a moodboard with all our thoughts and emotions for the upcoming season. Sometimes these ideas are mixed between the main collection and the lingerie line. That's normal because these are all the things you have in your head.

'We do this when we feel that it is appropriate. We never say, "oh, we have to make some outfits to show the lingerie" – it always has to feel natural. We never force ourselves to show the lingerie line.

PHOTOGRAPHY AND STYLING

'We do the styling, and the photography is always by Ronald Stoops. We've worked with him from the start. He was the first to work with the Antwerp Six designers from 1980 onwards. He has the ability to capture power and fragility in one image.'

'Our muse is the German artist Joseph Beuys and this red cross appears a lot in his work. It is a universal symbol, so it can be understood all over the world. We also adore uniforms, or the power of a uniform, so this red cross is a symbol — the language of the uniform, the language of the red cross.'

clockwise from top left:
University, Spring/Summer 2008;
Andres Sarda, Spring/Summer 2008;
University, Spring/Summer 2008

Andres Sarda ⤬

With a background as a textile engineer, Andrés Sardá creates lingerie with a sculptural simplicity that belies the technical skills behind the innovative fabrics and the precision of its manufacture. Starting up in conservative 1960s Spain, Andres Sarda is now a worldwide label; its design inheritance is carried on by Andrés' daughter, Núria.

Although Andrés Sardá is in his late seventies, he is still very much involved in the brand. He works part-time for the company, while for the last ten years his daughter Núria has been in charge of design and his son-in-law Carlos has looked after marketing and communication. Andrés Sardá, who likes to call his work 'mode intime', was the first designer to use stretch lace in lingerie, creating the first Leavers lace with Lycra. Núria gave the interview.

'My grandfather started a textile business in Barcelona, making lace. He then expanded into manufacturing lace mantillas, used by women at that time principally for going to church. His son, my father Andrés Sardá, studied as a textile engineer before working at Sardá Hermanos, the mantilla-making side of the business.

'My father was charged with launching the Sarda mantillas into the United States, Central and South America. He proved extremely successful, even having his mantillas worn by Jackie Kennedy. However, the mantilla business took a severe dip in sales from the 1960s onwards, as the Vatican was believed (although it was never clearly stated) to have proclaimed the wearing of the mantilla to church as no longer compulsory.

'It was in 1962 that my father decided to launch his first lingerie collection. He called it *Risk*, because it was really a risk for us to move from ecclesiastical mantillas to lingerie! My father said that at that time, during the Franco years, we only had Spanish products in the shops; lingerie was rather orthopaedic and only functional, and he wanted to make something more elegant for women. It was always important for him that the product was made for women to enjoy wearing.'

THE ANDRES SARDA WOMAN
⤬

'The Sarda woman has a strong, independent mind; she knows what she wants and if she wants something, she will buy it. She dresses for herself first, not just for a man. She cannot be imagined as one person, so we try to create a collection that works for a wide range of women. We want anyone who wants to wear our lingerie to be able to find a design that's right for them.'

THE DESIGN PROCESS
⤬

'We start with a resumé of the last season. We look at what was successful and then we think what we would like to find or develop. There's not just one thing that inspires us. You can be inspired when you travel, when you go to the cinema, and so on. I think you pick up many influences every day, in many situations, but you are not always conscious of them.

'We then work with our suppliers to develop special fabrics from the ideas we have. Sometimes it works, sometimes it doesn't; you have something in your mind, but it's not real and when it arrives, maybe it's okay, maybe not. It's a

lot of work to develop these fabrics, but then you do have really special things. We have to start the process really early, to be able to make all the changes we need to arrive at the right product.'

FAVOURITE FABRICS

'Lace is very important. Also we work a lot with silk, all types of silk. We like to work with people who supply the haute couture houses and high-end prêt-à-porter. Because they are not involved with lingerie, they make new and different things for us.'

FAVOURITE DESIGNS

'It is very difficult to single one out, because there are many things that my father did that I think are incredible. The invisible bra that he designed in the 1970s, after evolving many times, is still in the range today.

'We were the first to use transparent plastic bra straps, on a silk bra. We also created bras made completely from PVC plastic. We designed a bra trimmed with diamonds, one trimmed with mink and also bras where the back was completely made up of chains of pearls or satin ribbon lacing.'

THE CATWALK SHOWS

'Every season, Andres Sarda creates a catwalk show as part of Madrid Fashion Week. We make special pieces for the event, because for us, it must be a proper show and we need it to be really spectacular. We count on a team of people to make the stage set, choose the music, and so on; we have people who come especially from New York just to create our catwalk. We also design dresses for the show, and all the shoes and accessories are made especially for the event. It is a lot of work for 20 minutes!

'It's hard to choose just one favourite show, but for me, our catwalk show *Cabaret*, from Autumn/Winter 2008, was very special. We all have different favourites: the *Orient Express*, *Africa*, *Gustav Klimt* and *Mood for Love* were collections that everybody loved.'

THE BOUTIQUES

'Andres Sarda has four boutiques in Spain: two in Madrid, one in Alicante and one in Marbella. For us, it is important to transmit the Sarda mood, to create a space where customers feel really great and where we can show the collections in the style we prefer. We like to display the collections in a very clean way, but not cold — sophisticated, rather. We are a small company, so we have all been involved in how the stores look and it is very important for us to get all the details right.'

clockwise from top left:
Sketch by Andrés Sardá; Marbella boutique; *Andres Sarda*,
Autumn/Winter 2008/09; sketch by Andrés Sardá; *Cabaret*
catwalk show, Autumn/Winter 2006/07; sketch by Andrés Sardá

'There are now three labels. Andres Sarda *is the top of the market, a really high-end product, high-end in everything — in fashion, in quality, in silhouette.* Risk *is also high-quality, but it's for a woman who takes fewer risks and is more understated.* University *is for the woman who wants the Sarda fashion look, but without it costing as much.'*

Bien Fée pour toi ⁓

Vanessa Schleimer is the designer behind the French label Bien Fée pour toi. Based in Paris, her style mixes the fresh, pure mountain spirit of the French Alps where she was born with a sexy but gamine 1950s pin-up style to create lingerie with a modern twist.

'After growing up in Aix-les-Bains in Savoy, I studied in Paris. I took a general design foundation course at Creapole and then studied fashion design at the Atelier Chardon Savard.

'When I finished my studies, I did work experience at several couture houses in Paris, including the Lagerfeld Gallery, and then designed a few fashion collections as a freelancer. Then I worked as an assistant stylist for the fashion pages of *Madame Figaro*, which was great fun. I went to the photoshoots and prepared everything, which means that I can now arrange all my own photography.

'All these experiences led me to feel that I was ready to have my own business. I then met my partner Pascal Reynaud, with whom I created Bien Fée pour toi. Pascal looks after the sales and marketing part of our business.

'The first Bien Fée pour toi collection was presented at the Salon International de la Lingerie in September 2005 and included corsetry and nightwear. The following season I added a homewear line and in time a range of accessories.'

THE INSPIRATION FOR THE DESIGNS
⁓

'My aim from the start was to free lingerie from a still rather prim look in colours and femininity. I have two key themes: freshness and fantasy. I'm inspired by the freshness and purity of nature, its small flowers and colours. I'll take a photo of a flower, for example and then, bit by bit, I bring it together with the fantasy side – I adore 1950s pin-ups, such as Marilyn Monroe, and also the fabulous Russian matryoshka dolls.

'The inspiration for a collection comes to me in a flash. I can have a sudden idea that I want to use violet, for example. It's not necessarily when I'm at the office. It can just be a detail and as soon as I think of it, I make notes, and voilà!'

THE BIEN FÉE POUR TOI WOMAN
⁓

'I act as a designer for people's moods. So I have very sexy lines, and others that are more romantic. I think I design equally well for a passionate and very feminine woman as for a woman who is more discreet and romantic. Every woman changes her mood and what she wants, so I have a broad palette of styles to give her a choice.

'I've worked for years with Spicy-box, two graphic designer friends who have created all my catalogues. They created the typography for the logo and a female designer added the wings. I really like the fact that you can create so many scrolling curves around the words. It's magical and ultra-feminine. It's a bit 1970s. It has evolved over time and become softer, but it has always had the little butterfly that creates the initial "F" with its wing.'

FAR LEFT TO RIGHT:
So Chic and its inspiration, Autumn/Winter 2008/09;
Smoking, Autumn/Winter 2009/10

PAST COLLECTIONS

'I think that in all my collections to date you find the same feelings of freshness, purity and softness. For example, we have this line *Un Ange Passe* ("An Angel Passes By") for someone who feels romantic and therefore very sensual. Each season I have a special silhouette; often it's the mini-skirt shortie. I adore this style — it's very pin-up and quite unusual, but very popular.'

THE FAVOURITE COLLECTION

'My favourite is the Winter 2008 collection and the line *Cabaret*. It's really everything that I love; it's both glamorous and delicate at the same time. It's a half-cup bra with a ruffled edge to the neckline and straps, worn with a knicker also edged with ruffles. It's in coral matt microfibre overlaid with chocolate-coloured lace. I really like this play of rather surprising mixes of colours and fabrics.'

FABRICS AND TRIMS

'I go to the fabric fairs to see the collections and I work on impulse — I might get a sudden impulse for a printed silk mousseline, for example. The fabrics come principally from France and also Europe. All my laces come from France, from Saint-André near Lyon. I am very loyal to them because their laces are both refined and very modern, and lace must look modern. I also find silk mousseline and printed cottons in France. I buy a lot from Italy and I source Liberty prints, which I adore, from England.

'I adore working with stretch satin and all the ultra-soft fabrics. The priority for me is that they must be very soft — silk, satin, Tactel, mircofibre and then the ultra-refined fabrics like lace and silk mousseline. For homewear, I prefer to use pointelle knits and printed cottons.'

PHOTOGRAPHY AND STYLING

'We have always worked with the American photographer Liz Giguère. We are really in tune with one another. I do the styling and I adore doing it. We do shoots in the studio, but I love doing photoshoots outside too.

'Recently we went back to my home region of Aix-les-Bains in Savoy. I adore doing photoshoots in the cornfields at dawn, or by the side of a lake. In the studio, I prefer to create small sets and it's nice to be able to change the background quickly this way. I enjoy going to get the small accessories, shoes and so on.'

clockwise from far left:

Un Ange Passé, Spring/Summer 2007; *Fantasy* sketch, Autumn/Winter 2007/08;
Double Je sketches and moodboard, Autumn/Winter 2006/07; *Fantasy*, Autumn/Winter 2007/08

clockwise from left:
Chameleon Girl, Spring/Summer 2007; *Lili Bulle*, Autumn/Winter 2009/10;
Pin-Up inspiration; *Divine*, Autumn/Winter 2009/10; *Pin-Up* inspiration

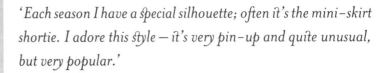

'Each season I have a special silhouette; often it's the mini-skirt shortie. I adore this style — it's very pin-up and quite unusual, but very popular.'

LEFT TO RIGHT:
Sketches by Carol Malony; *Rainbow Bright*, Spring/Summer 2009;
Champagne Taste, Autumn/Winter 2008 (winner of the Ultra Modernity award)

Carol Malony ❧

From introducing French lingerie to Los Angeles in the 1970s to creating statement outfits for the stars of 1980s movies and television, Carol Malony now combines these two loves to create modern Hollywood glamour with an irreverent glance at the Tinseltown pin-ups of the 1950s.

'I was born in Toronto, Canada, and when I was seven my father packed up the entire family and moved to California. I graduated in philosophy from college in Santa Cruz and moved to San Francisco working in a crazy admin job dealing with rock stars, such as Van Morrison.

'In 1973, my aunt May called to tell me about the tragic demise of my uncle — a sales representative for all the French lingerie companies selling in Toronto. I thought, "Why don't we take all that beautiful lingerie and do something with it in Los Angeles?" — because there was nothing like it in the whole area. My husband had just graduated from architectural school and my father was a graphic artist, so they designed and built the store and I imported French lingerie via Canada.

'The space in the shopping mall in Woodland Hills was very long, with a lot of empty space at the back, so it was the perfect idea to go and get my grandfather's sewing machines from Toronto. I wanted to start designing things that weren't being done, like D cups and nude colours and also, there was a 48% import tariff on everything. Pretty soon there were 26 sewers in this back room with cutting tables and sewing machines everywhere. Customers would come in and I'd have all the things displayed artistically on the wall; we were doing couture! We would take things in, rip things out, pad one side — it was this kind of practicality that brought me into all of this, without realizing how unusual it was.

'Stylists came in and that led to doing all sorts of film and television work. My most fun project was the TV show *Dallas*. One story line involved Sue Ellen developing a lingerie business, so every week I was doing more and more lingerie for the show. *Fringe a Go-Go*, my best-selling piece right now, has its roots in my famous white fringe bodysuit from *Dallas*. That led to *Knots Landing* and *Falcon Crest*, and I also did some work with stars like Dolly Parton, Cher and Pat Benetar. I opened a second store in the heart of Beverly Hills and my clients became people like Debbie Reynolds — really *Beverly Hills 90210*.

'I ended up with four stores, but I sold them because I liked designing better. I started focusing more on the manufacturing and private label business. Victoria's Secret ended up having most of my time, and I designed for the Fashion & Glamour category, including many of the catalogue cover pieces and best-sellers.

'In 2007 I decided to give it another shot and put the label on the market. I had a bunch of young people working with me who all really wanted to do it. I took the product line to the Paris lingerie show Salon International de la Lingerie for the first time in January 2008, and I won the Ultra Modernity award.'

THE CAROL MALONY WOMAN

'The first thing I think about is my own physical reaction to what I'm doing. It has to get an emotional reaction; "Wow, that's really beautiful, look at that!" I don't do things that you just say "Oh well" to.

'This woman is going to walk out of the dressing room with a different posture than when she came in. I might not be able to educate her, cure her or finance her, but I can make her feel better about herself!

'Lingerie gives you permission to express yourself in another language. It can be beautifully done, it can be articulate, it can be poetic — it can be sexy! It's really a language to communicate.'

THE INSPIRATIONS FOR THE DESIGNS

'I seldom have an idea before I find the materials. It can start with a charm or even a bow and you just build it up. Sometimes it starts with an idea and then you have to find the materials to do it, but I always find that's like filling in. It's much better to start with materials and drape them on a stand so that they find their own dramatic style.

'I take the fabrics, laces and embroideries and drape the shapes, take pictures of them and then take these to a pattern-maker. I've always worked with a team; a pattern-maker and cutter and a few really good sewers. I like to dye things in the sink and put them together and make things up. We challenge ourselves to do the unusual.'

THE COLLABORATION

'With the people I work with, everyone can get involved. I could turn around to anyone in my studio, even the postman who walks in, and ask "which bow do you like best?" You can share it. What I love about what I do is that it's a collaboration; there's a buzz, an energy.'

FAVOURITE DESIGNS

'The bodysuit launched me, at the time when innerwear as outerwear became a real phenomenon. I think I sold about a million garments to Victoria's Secret. I would see women wearing them at cocktail bars or clubs — which is fun for a lingerie designer, because normally you don't see the garments. Now I make sure that there is something in every group that says, "I can wear this out!"

'Recently, probably the best pieces for me are Barely There. *It's the quintessential mix between tradition and fashion — New World / Old World, antique/fresh. I really do think it's the perfect bra.'*

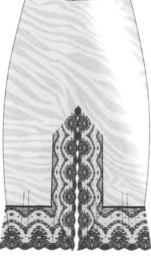

clockwise from near right:
Hollywood inspiration moodboard; sketch by
Carol Malony; *Barely There*, Spring/Summer 2008;
Fringe a Go-Go, Autumn/Winter 2008/09;
Prom Night, Autumn/Winter 2009/10

Chantal Thomass ⌘

Chantal Thomass has a strong recognizable style of her own — the tailored trouser suit, black bob, black eyelashes and matt scarlet lips. Look carefully and this chic Parisienne style contains small touches of Chantal's favourite lingerie details — a tiny embroidery scallop edge or a small frill of eyelash-fringed lace.

clockwise from top left:
'Secrets —The Lure of Lingerie', St. Gallen Textile Museum; *Merveilleuse*, Spring/Summer 2008; *Doll'ita*, Autumn/Winter 2008/09

Painted a classic dove grey with white accents, Chantal's Paris boutique reflects her love of classic French decorative motifs, such as rococo medallions and swags, which have been translated into prints or jacquard designs.

Chantal Thomass grew up on the outskirts of Paris, and by the age of eighteen had already started designing outfits for herself and her friends. As a reaction against the rather formal 'grown-up' fashion of the 1950s and early 60s, Chantal's style fused child-like elements with the rustic—ethnic hippy look. Chantal started her own label, Ter et Bantine, in 1967, designing quirky collections that betrayed even then the playful spirit that has become her signature style.

In 1975 Chantal Thomass started designing under her own name and brought out her first lingerie collections. 'In the 1960s and 70s while feminists were burning their bras, it wasn't at all fashionable to wear lingerie. I hadn't paid any attention to it up until then and all of a sudden, when I was about twenty/twenty-five, I wanted to wear it.

'I discovered through books and films the lingerie of the 1930s and 40s, and I adored it. I made it for myself at first and then for a catwalk show, but just as an accessory to the fashion. For my Autumn/Winter 1976/77 show, I started the catwalk with girls in suits with white accessories and around them one girl in white broderie anglaise lingerie. All the photos published of the show were of the one girl in lingerie!'

Chantal's lingerie was quickly taken up by the press, and the lingerie pieces that she had designed as accessories to her fashion line — corsets, balconette bras and suspender belts — began to fly out of her boutique on Paris's trendy Left Bank.

From 1980, Chantal designed lingerie collections in her own name, but in 1995 her business partners cancelled her contract and she was unable to use her own name for three years. In 1998, Chantal signed a partnership agreement with the Dim group, allowing her to return to lingerie.

Chantal Thomass lingerie is available worldwide. She has a boutique in Paris, a boutique in Moscow and in addition to the lingerie, collections of hosiery, swimwear, umbrellas and a range of perfumes and toiletries. The black-and-white silhouette theme started when Chantal met the media designer Benoît Devarieux.

THE INSPIRATIONS FOR THE DESIGNS
⌘

'It can be anything; an image in a book or a magazine, a film, a girl in the street, anything. I like the element of dance, parties and festivals; I've designed bustiers with huge tutu skirts. I'm very inspired by the dresses of tango dancers.

LEFT TO RIGHT:
Malicieuse, Spring/Summer 2008;
Sweet Poker, Autumn/Winter
2008/09; 'Secrets – The Lure
of Lingerie', St. Gallen Textile
Museum (both images)

*'I adore vintage lingerie. I often go to flea markets, especially when I'm travelling, in New York,
London, everywhere. I've got an enormous vintage collection.'*

'I prefer to design my ready-to-wear with inspiration taken from lingerie, such as broderie anglaise or corsets. I like the masculine/feminine element, the contrast between the suit, which is something I'm well-known for, and lingerie.'

Chantal curated an exhibition of vintage lingerie at the St. Gallen Textile Museum, Switzerland, in 2008 that included pieces from her own collection.

FAVOURITE FABRICS

'I like the transparency of lace, especially very fine Chantilly lace. I really like satin and the transparency of tulle. I like to visit the suppliers' factories — the lace factories at Calais, Como in Italy for prints and St. Gallen in Switzerland for embroidery.'

THE BOUTIQUE

The new Chantal Thomass boutique opened in 2004 on rue Saint-Honoré, right next door to the super-cool Colette.

'I was looking to create a boudoir, trying to make it warm and cosy but at the same time contemporary using modern materials. The pink is a mid-tone between black and white, and pink is such a beautiful colour as it reflects and gives your skin a lovely glow, especially when you're undressed!

'I worked together with the designer Christian Ghion. I brought all the feminine side to it; he brought all the contemporary materials, such as the Corian columns and the pink transparent Dacryl furniture. We mixed it up — for example, the Dacryl tables with Louis Quinze feet.

'Benoît Devarieux worked on the whole campaign, communicating through me. Over the next few years, he always took photos of me, soft focus, in strange situations, doing quite funny things. We were working on the silhouette with the photographer. By chance it created a Chinese shadow effect of me leaning against the chair, and Benoît turned me into a logo!'

clockwise from top left:
Sweet Poker, Autumn/Winter 2008/09; *Bas à la Ancienne*,
Autumn/Winter 2008/09; Chantal Thomass boutique
interior; boutique exterior, rue Saint-Honoré, Paris

LEFT TO RIGHT:
Helena collection sketch; *Helena* collection; *Fairies* collection sketch

Claire Pettibone ❧

Claire Pettibone designs lingerie spun from a romanticism of a bygone age. Her childhood study of ballet helped shape her ideas of femininity and taught her how to create an effect of effortless, ethereal beauty through hard work and determination.

'When I was a child we moved to rural New York, to a nineteenth-century house filled with clothes from its previous owner, who had been quite a fashion plate in the 1920s. She had beaded flapper gowns and purses; it was like a treasure hunt going through all of her things. My parents are both artists, so I was exposed to art and creativity from a very young age.

'As a teenager, I developed an interest in fashion and loved looking at European fashion magazines, with their fantastic images of glamorous, strong and feminine women. I studied fashion design at Otis-Parsons School of Design in Los Angeles. My senior portfolio consisted of lingerie and evening gowns; these categories allowed me to express my romantic, feminine style.

'My first job was as the design assistant to one of my college professors, who was the senior designer for a lingerie company. Within a year, she left and I was promoted to senior designer. I stayed there for five years before meeting my future husband, Guy Toley. Guy worked in finance and film production and wanted to start a business, and I had ideas for design, so we began …

'At the time we launched our business, European lingerie was very special, but extremely expensive once imported to the US. Most American companies were producing very bland, utilitarian products. I wanted to offer an exquisite, vintage-inspired collection to the American market. I reintroduced many of the lost techniques (such as handmade ribbon flowers and vintage lace patterns) that I'd found on antique pieces, but updated them for the modern woman.'

THE CLAIRE PETTIBONE WOMAN
❧

'All women are beautiful, and it is my job to enhance that beauty with clothing. I see lingerie as an opportunity to step "out of time", take a moment for oneself and perhaps share it with someone special. I may create a fantasy of lounging in a beautiful home, drinking champagne, eating whipped cream and berries while draped in beautiful lingerie! It's not reality, but I imagine my clients living this life of luxury.'

THE INSPIRATIONS FOR THE COLLECTIONS
❧

'First would be all eras of costume history, from nineteenth-century lace and 1920s clothing and accessories to 1940s wallpaper. Next would be nature and flowers, birds, butterflies, clouds … the natural world is such a rich tapestry of colour and design. In addition, I studied ballet from the age of eight through sixteen. The rich history, delicate costumes and romanticism helped shape my ideas of femininity and beauty. I often choose a theme for the season and research and collect objects related to that theme as a starting point for developing a collection. Past themes have included *Fairies*, *Goddesses*, *Angels*, *The Language of Flowers*, and *Shakespeare in Love*.'

THE DESIGN PROCESS
⁓

'It starts with the fabrics. I play with combinations of textures and colours; I may have a particular treatment or silhouette in mind. The next challenge is finding that perfect combination of elements that go into a piece of lingerie. It's quite complex when you consider all of the fabrics and trimmings involved, and I really enjoy seeing the pieces come together.

'I go to New York and Paris to source fabrics and trims, and we also have an excellent textile fair here in Los Angeles where I see many of my European vendors. Every collection begins with a first sample made up in the studio, then changes are made from there and the collection evolves to the finished product.

'We make everything in Los Angeles. We take great pride in being one of the few companies to support our local economy and still have things made in the US. We like to have our eye on things here so that we can maintain our quality and the integrity of the design.'

THE LINGERIE AND THE BRIDAL COLLECTIONS
⁓

'There is an underlying femininity and romance in all of my work. I have developed quite a speciality for lace and embroideries, so there is a relationship there. The thought process is similar, in that the goal is to make a woman look absolutely breathtaking. Lingerie can be a bit playful and, of course, is not as serious as a wedding gown, so there is a lightness that goes into creating the lingerie.'

PAST COLLECTIONS
⁓

'My first collection was called *Luna*. It had beautiful silk ribbon passementerie work. *Honeysuckle* was a delicate Chantilly lace, very vintage-feeling. For the *Inanna* collection we sprinkled flowers on layered tulle.

'The *Athena* collection has become my signature collection and has been in the line for many years. It features ornate guipure lace and continues to be a favourite. I love rich embroideries with elaborate border details as in the *Helena* collection.'

PHOTOGRAPHY AND STYLING
⁓

'I'm the creative director and we produce all of our ad campaigns in-house. I choose the photographer, select the models and plan the styling and mood of each shoot. I start with a point of inspiration and build the story from there. One of my favourites is *Year of the Goddess*. I did a lot of research on goddesses from all cultures, and each collection was named after a different one. We styled the shoot to be very iconic of that beautiful but strong ideal of womanhood.'

THE BOUTIQUE
⁓

'We've been open since 2001. The boutique has exposed wood beam ceilings, with my collection of crystal chandeliers and flowers hanging from the rafters. It's filled with some of my favourite antique furniture and it has an eclectic, very feminine vibe.'

CLOCKWISE FROM ABOVE:
Inspiration for the *Goddess* collection, 1999; *Goddess*, 1999; inspiration for the *Fairies* collection; *Blossom* from the *Fairies* collection; *Honeysuckle* sketch

Honeysuckle chemise

Antoinette
gown
&
Robe

clockwise from top left:
The Beverly Hills boutique; *Juliet* bridal collection; *Antoinette* collection robe and gown;
Athena sketch; *Athena* collection

Elise Anderegg ✦

Paris-based Elise Anderegg draws on her knowledge of couture and the tradition of French lace to create lingerie that incorporates references from the past, but is designed to be worn in a truly modern way. Moods and influences often reference the atmospheric storyboards of French cinema, both contemporary and classic.

'I was born in Switzerland, in the French-speaking Jura mountain region. I was always interested in fashion and I started out at an arts school in Switzerland, studying fashion management for haute couture. I came to Paris when I was twenty to study at the ESMOD fashion school, specializing in luxury and couture. I didn't think about lingerie at the time, only about making beautiful things, in beautiful fabrics, with beautiful silhouettes.

'After ESMOD, I worked for the French lace company Solstiss. I looked after the Paris area, working with couture houses such as Chanel, Ungaro and Louis Vuitton to develop laces for them.

'I had always wanted to create something for myself and I liked the idea of creating a small label. I'd always loved babydoll nightdresses worn over jeans and things like that, but I think it was being introduced to lace as a fabric that led me to drift into lingerie, almost in spite of myself. It's such a noble, light fabric with its play of transparency.

'When in 2003 I came to create my brand, I wasn't thinking, "I'm designing lingerie". What emerged was very light, and very much derived from lingerie, but at the same time you couldn't say it was traditional lingerie. The first collection was very innerwear/outerwear — really very close to prêt-à-porter. Gradually I evolved into making lingerie and today I make both lingerie and corsetry.

'I was only twenty-five and perhaps a bit naïve. At the start, you have a rather creative vision; I wanted to make people dream a little through my collections and my photographs. I did everything by myself and it worked out quite easily.'

THE ELISE ANDEREGG WOMAN
✦

'I think of a woman who's quite romantic and likes wearing pretty things, but when she is in the mood will dare to wear really fine lingerie.'

FAVOURITE SILHOUETTES
✦

'The silhouettes I like most are rather romantic and slightly flirtatious, but not suggestive. I really love transparency, and often have an element of transparency on the camisoles and lingerie. I use very pretty fabrics, but they are never too suggestive; it really stops at flirtatious. It's the babydoll that's really my silhouette, worn simply over jeans with a great pair of heels.

'The key pieces that return every season are the babydolls and the camisoles that you can wear as inner or outerwear. They work well in the collection, always with little lace details.

'I really love references from the 1930s, when women were slightly more emancipated, very *garçonne*, but at the same time very sensual. I like women

left to right:
Retro influence; Spring/Summer 2008;
Criminalmente Bella, Autumn/Winter 2008/09

to be womanly and I don't like anything at all
vulgar; you can very quickly fall into bad taste
with lingerie. What interests me is making a
woman beautiful.'

THE DESIGN PROCESS

'I do a lot of my work at the fabric show Première
Vision, because a lot of the suppliers I see there
work for both lingerie and luxury prêt-à-porter.
It's really important that the concept starts at the
beginning there.'

FAVOURITE FABRICS

'My favourite fabrics are laces. I really like
Chantilly laces because of their transparent
qualities. At the moment I love cotton, macramé-
style laces too. I also like mousseline, chiffons,
and anything in silk and satins — I work with
them every season. 80 per cent of my fabrics are
French, the rest are Italian.

'I love anything that looks a bit old-fashioned. I've
worked with cotton laces from Calais with a matt
appearance. There's no shine in them at all and
they're a little bit "crude", but they really give the
bra a vintage feel — with a modern silhouette, of
course. I prefer to have a natural fabric on a bra.'

PHOTOGRAPHY AND STYLING

'First of all, I have lots of ideas for the mood
that I want to create. I often use references
from cinema; I really love aspects of mainstream
cinema. For example, with the catalogue for the
Summer 2009 collection, I used influences
from the French film *L'Été Meurtrier* ("One Deadly
Summer"). It's a film from the early 1980s with a
young Isabelle Adjani, who is very sexy and arrives
from Paris and the people in the countryside
don't know what to think — she is really a *femme
fatale*. We shot our photographs in the countryside
around Paris and I placed all the models outside
in run-down summerhouses, in the woods or
by a lake.

'I prefer to have strong statements in my photography, where there are these references. I do the
styling and Julien Benassi is my artistic director;
he is also the graphic designer responsible for the
catalogues. I've worked with the same photographer,
Fabrice Mabillot, for four years. We've kept the
same really good team.'

clockwise from above:
Secret, Autumn/Winter 2009/10; sketches and patterns; *Couture*, Autumn/Winter 2009/10

clockwise from top left:
Fabric details; *Couture*, Autumn/Winter 2009/10; *Songes D'Été*,
Spring/Summer 2009; *Séduction*, Spring/Summer 2009;
lace sample; *Elise*, cotton tulle and cotton lace; lace sample

clockwise from top left:
Queen Sauvage, Spring/Summer 2009;
inspiration — vintage moodboard with
faded colours; *Chipie*, Spring/Summer
2008; *Orient Excess*, Autumn/Winter
2008/09

Elise Aucouturier ✦

From her home in the historic town of Chantilly outside Paris, Elise Aucouturier designs lingerie that is both modern and timeless. Elise's sophisticated eye for fabrics allows her to mix traditional elements with the newest fabric blends to create sensuously luxurious pieces.

'I was born in Paris and I was always interested in fashion, from a small child, but not necessarily lingerie. My parents weren't involved with fashion at all, but my maternal grandmother was a milliner — she had an atelier in Paris making hats — and my paternal grandmother was a lingerie designer/maker. She worked from home, as people used to, and therefore she kept in the loft all the styles that she had done in the past. When I went to her house in the holidays, my cousin and I spent entire days rummaging through the loft trying on the old corsets and cotton embroidered pyjamas — it was great fun!

'I studied fashion at ESMOD in Paris and chose to specialize in lingerie. It was the first year in which lingerie was offered as an option. After my degree, I started working straight away for different lingerie brands to learn the business. I had always wanted to have my own company, but I wanted to work for a while, to find out how things worked, to get to know the fabrics and the fabric suppliers.

'I worked for five years for companies such as Vanity Fair and at design houses such as Christian Dior and Marîthé et François Girbaud. I really saw the different sides of the business. Then I became pregnant and as I wanted to look after my children myself, I stopped working for two years. Then in 2001, I created my brand.'

THE INSPIRATIONS FOR THE DESIGNS
✦

'Everything! It could be people in the street; it could be a fashion image from a magazine, something from the cinema or something seen while I'm travelling. It's like being a sponge soaking up ideas.

'My favourite fashion designers also inspire me. I always look to see what they are doing. I love Jean-Paul Gaultier for the way he mixes fabrics and colours and his colour harmonies.'

THE DESIGN PROCESS
✦

'Primarily it starts with the fabrics. I go to the Paris textile fair Première Vision to choose my fabrics. It's often the fabrics that give me the style for the collection, and that give me the colour mood — it's the departure point.

'I visit Première Vision because for me it's more interesting to be inspired by prêt-à-porter trends, by prêt-à-porter fabrics and prêt-à-porter colours than to go looking at a lingerie fabric fair for things that aren't necessarily adapted to what I do and are too focused on corsetry or lingerie.'

FAVOURITE COLLECTIONS
✦

'I really like a line called *Cachez-moi à Minuît*. It was my first line and it sold really well. It was a "combinette" style, a short chemise in jersey, with lace bands

'My collections are made in France. I work with different specialist ateliers; some who do jersey, some who do more woven fabrics, and so on.'

clockwise from top left:
Queen Sauvage, Spring/Summer 2009;
sketch by Elise Aucouturier;
Falbala Tzar, Spring/Summer 2009;
Queen Sauvage, Spring/Summer 2009

edging the cups, under the bust and around the hem. It was very simple, very architectural, very pure, and so, consequently, it was very modern.

'I've used the shape again, but modified it. For example, in the line *My Tour Eiffel* I took the idea of the bands but I added other details to make the design more sophisticated. This design was taken up by a lot of brands at the time. I'm rather proud of this — it's better to be copied than be a copier! It was also the theme, the commercial formula that launched my brand.'

FAVOURITE FABRICS

'I would say that 90 per cent of the fabrics come from France; all the laces are from Calais or from Caudry, the embroideries come from Switzerland and the cottons from Switzerland or Italy.

'My favourite fabric isn't silk or lace. What I really love, personally, are the new blends of jerseys. For example, jerseys blended with cashmere — the knitted fabric is really nice and soft — or styles in bamboo mixed with silk; they are luxurious, but at the same time not necessarily luxurious to the eye. It's not obvious luxury, very high-shine and silky; this luxury is in the touch, the handle, not in how it looks.'

PHOTOGRAPHY AND STYLING

'I don't like photos that are too "finished" or too much like a catalogue. For me, it's very important that first of all the photos interpret a mood and that they have an artistic sensibility — that comes before the commercial angle.

'The styling is like a reward. When you've worked on a collection with all the difficulties involved, it's rewarding to have it worn by a pretty model and shown off beautifully by a photographer. It's a real pleasure.'

clockwise from left:
Falbala Tzar, Spring/Summer 2009; *Falbala Tzar*, Spring/Summer
2009; *Poupée des Songes*, Spring/Summer 2009; *Queen Sauvage*,
Spring/Summer 2009

MOULIN ROUGE CONCERT
MOULIN ROUGE BAL
MOULIN ROUGE TOUS LES SOIRS
LA GOULUE

TOUS LES SOIRS
MOULIN ROUGE
les Mercredis et Samedis
BAL MASQUÉ

Eva Rachline ~

The lingerie designs of Parisian Eva Rachline are infused with the bohemian spirit of theatre, cinema and cabaret. Growing up in a world of stage sets and celluloid glamour, Eva translates her influences into colourful pieces that mix fabrics, laces and embroideries in a modern approach to lingerie.

clockwise from top left:
The Paris boutique; *Papillon*, Autumn/Winter 2008/09; *Liaison* collection sketch; inspiration from the world of Toulouse-Lautrec

'I first became interested in fashion very early on. When I was eleven, my friend and I started designing bikinis in Liberty cotton prints. I created very simple pieces with cord ties and we sold them to relations and friends.

'I grew up in Paris. Both my parents are in the arts; my father was an interior decorator and my mother was a head set designer for films. In their studios, there were stage sets, fabrics everywhere, scale models, furnishing fabrics, elaborately worked fabrics, paintings, jacquards with amazing yarns; it was a whole universe that managed to be both eighteenth century and cinematic at the same time.

'I often went on location shoots with my mother and since then film has always been an influence, something magical. As a child, I used to go to the cinema five times a week. I saw every film – it really was a passion. Theatre too; we regularly went to the Comédie-Française. My parents took me everywhere and when we travelled we always went to see an opera, a play or a musical.

'I studied fashion at ESMOD in Paris. In my final year, we had the opportunity to enter three competitions. I won prizes in all three, including awards for Vanity Fair lingerie and Calais lace – and every time, it was lingerie I was designing.

'After ESMOD, I worked as a lingerie designer for different companies. But I had always wanted my independence, so I set up my own company in 1991, working freelance, so that I could launch my label, which I did in 1996.'

THE EVA RACHLINE WOMAN
~

'She has a certain elegance – not a classic elegance, but a unique elegance that stems from her personality and appears through her way of dressing. Looking at this woman, with her independent spirit, it allows me to turn lingerie into an accessory that completes her outfit. It's a vision of a woman who is very modern, but who appreciates the rather retro appeal of good quality.'

THE INSPIRATIONS FOR THE DESIGNS
~

'The original creative world in which I grew up still inspires me today. The films that I loved, the people I met, the travelling we did; it's a whole mixed-up story that comes out in my collections. Now there are contemporary inspirations, too: interiors, books, exhibitions and paintings. I love the world of Toulouse-Lautrec; the colours, the movement, the composition.'

THE DESIGN PROCESS
~

'Everything starts with the fabric. I have an idea of shape, often not very specific, but the trigger is the fabric – when I see the fabric, everything starts going. I immediately get ideas about colours and mixes (of colour and fabric) that I want to use, then everything falls into place; it's almost methodical.

clockwise from top left:
New York collection sketches; *Pirate guêpière*, *Liaison* collection;
sketches, fabrics and trims for *Boudoir* collection

HYDRA

HELOISE

'It's a whole story that's being created, using the same code to choose colour, finishes, details. Influences may come from the Directoire period, as well as from the eighteenth century or from cabaret. Afterwards, I work on the key silhouettes and on the other items than come from them, because I now make many pieces that complement the lingerie, such as little bolero jackets, cashmere armwarmers and stockings.'

FAVOURITE COLLECTIONS

'In general, I like my winter collections more than my summer collections, because they are a more compressed, strong and edited version of everything that I love. With summer it is more difficult for me to find my dream, although I do love my collection *Lubitsch*, named after the film director, and *Ludwig* was also a line I really adored.

'My favourite is the collection that's coming next; it's still fresh and new, but not for long. In design, a moment goes by and you pass onto something else. So, past collections are a bit past it! But my previous collections always feature the play of fabrics, the play of contrasts and of details. Everything is in the finishing touches. It's these little things that make the difference.'

FAVOURITE DESIGN

'We have a bustier that comes back season after season. It's generally in silk and lace; I review and change the laces. What's special about it is that it's very comfortable — you can wear it all day, as innerwear or as outerwear, as part of your outfit.'

THE BOUTIQUE

'The boutique was a dream come true! It's rather like a stage set and gives the brand a beautiful backdrop. I found this place by chance; it's an eighteenth-century building. I loved it straightaway — a *coup de coeur*. I loved the façade. It's from the early nineteenth century and it's one of the last few that remain in the street. I loved its rather quirky side; the floor slopes, the walls are all rather odd. It has a lot of charm.

'We've been here since 2004 and we have done a lot of work to the space. I wanted to create a touch of theatre, but with a certain modernity. I played a lot with the idea of the world of the stage, a spectacular — as if you were entering a cabaret salon.

'All the contrasts I love are here, using quite modern finishes such as the blocks of silver — the silver leaf of the façade, the bureau and cash desk. There are three key colours: a theatrical red, a soft and romantic parma violet and silver, a material I love. The blocks of silver really jump out against the rough stonework of the walls.'

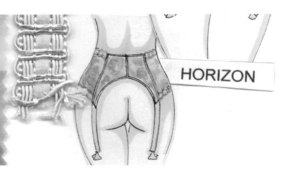

HORIZON

clockwise from top left:
The Paris boutique; fabrics and trims for the *Liaison* collection; *Satine*
camisole from *Liaison* collection; sketches for the *Liaison* collection;
Senteur zip top from the *Ludwig* collection

La belle époque

Fifi Chachnil ⤗

Fifi Chachnil is Paris lingerie personified in its forever gamine and girlish glamour. From a background in the closely linked worlds of fashion and art in 1980s Paris, Fifi has created a label that epitomizes boudoir lingerie, based on her own vision of the purest form of femininity.

TOP TO BOTTOM:

Inspiration; Fifi Chachnil and her three daughters

'I became interested in lingerie when I was very young. I went to a girls' school in Paris where you wore the same uniform from kindergarten until you left. The only way I could personalize my uniform was with lingerie – I shortened my skirt so much that you could see my panty.

'After school I went to Clevcland, Ohio, to study graphic design. I then came back to Paris and tried fashion school. I stayed only three months, as I didn't like the heavy commercial element. I took a trip to Egypt and loved the songs I heard there, so I became an Egyptian singer and made a record in Paris, complete with a dancing costume of bra and veils.

'I then started to design fashion collections, but I did it only for catwalk shows or for exhibitions in places like the Pompidou Centre. In 1984 I started working with the artists Pierre et Gilles on stage costumes and outfits for photoshoots. It wasn't lingerie at this stage, but it was so over-the-top that lingerie was always an important part – the dresses were extremely short, so naturally the knickers were on show. I made knickers with frills and underskirts to make the skirts stick out. So I've always made lingerie, but without saying that I did.

'In 1995 I decided I wanted to make lingerie. The idea was to make a lingerie collection that did not compromise on style. It was like fashion, but to wear underneath. It was very easily understood and took off straight away.'

THE INSPIRATIONS FOR THE DESIGNS
⤗

'Girls inspire me – their differences and singularity are my inspiration; the shape of the body and the way girls of different countries behave. Creativity often comes out of necessity.

'I'm inspired by the most feminine images from every era; women in their purest feminine form. The era of the Directoire, the Incroyables and the Merveilleuses, when women appeared virtually nude under transparent linen dresses, almost like nightdresses – this is an era that fascinates me, where women knew how to play with proportions.'

FAVOURITE COLLECTIONS
⤗

'The first! Because it was so well received I remember it very fondly. Some of the items that were in this first collection are still present now, such as the *Lisette* slip dress and the *Minette* panty, which is very tiny in the front but very covered in the back. We have girls who come back to buy this item again and again. I think that if you become attached to a label that makes a piece that you love, you want to find it there every time.'

clockwise from top left:
Boutique, rue Saint-Honoré, Paris;
design sketch; inspiration from the most
feminine images of every era; *Epatante*, from
Poupée collection, powder-pink cotton,
Autumn/Winter 2008/09

THE BABYDOLL SILHOUETTE

'This silhouette that I always work with is almost Incroyables or Merveilleuses-inspired, with an empire bustline. When I started, I was heavily pregnant. It wasn't a question of having different clothes; it was a question of being able to become pregnant and wear the same ones, to allow a woman to be ultra-feminine. This shape allows it.'

THE DESIGN PROCESS

'Everything depends on the fabric and that's what inspires me — the very first touch. It has to be as soft as possible and then the colour has to be decided very precisely. Only when I have chosen the fabric can I begin to draw. The drawing is therefore only an interpretation of the feeling given by the fabric.

'I go to fabric fairs, but the fabric suppliers often come here. I am very loyal; I prefer to work with suppliers that I know and have us work on things together. I also go to the fairs to discover unexpected things — I love to be surprised. My fabrics come mainly from the north of France, especially Calais and Caudry for the lace, while the silks come from Lyon in the south.'

THE BOUTIQUES

'In 1984 I set up my first boutique on rue Jean-Jacques Rousseau. We expanded the place in 1986 and in 1995. I imagined the boutique like a cosy girl's bedroom — you need to have surroundings that are "dressed" when you are getting undressed. The boutique on rue Saint-Honoré opened in 2002; there we are exactly where our real clients live and shop.'

THE LOGO

'It was originally a blue logo and just called "Chachnil", which was the stage name I took when I was doing Egyptian music. I just used my surname, not my first name. Delphine is my real name, so Fifi is easy to understand — it's very Paris, very lingerie; it's Moulin Rouge and cancans. Both logos were created by graphic designer Charles Petit.'

COLLABORATIONS WITH RETAILERS

'This passion for *savoir faire* and fine workmanship is interesting, but sometimes it's limiting to be able to reach only the clients who can afford to buy these pretty things. I've done several collaborations with retailers like Etam and La Redoute. This way you can produce large quantities and offer lower prices for young women who can't afford to buy my main line — it's democratic. I've also done a line for Topshop, which launched in September 2008.'

THE PERFUME

'Fifi fragrance is an unconventional perfume of intense femininity, with all the contradictions it implies: fancy and subtle, with almost masculine deep notes; insolence and tenderness. It starts lightly on the spicy notes of citrus fruits and coriander mixed to the powdered sweetness of rose. Amber brings its oriental harmony, spiced up insolently by tobacco. In the tradition of the great classics, its surprising harmonies sound in a natural way.'

clockwise from top left:
Details from the Fifi Chachnil boutique, rue Jean-Jacques Rousseau, Paris; *Fifi Chachnil for Topshop*, Autumn/Winter 2008/09 (both images)

fishbelly ❧

Jutta Teschner is the designer behind fishbelly. Based in Berlin's trendy Mitte district, she creates modern lingerie pieces that play with the city's history as a hotbed of racy 1930s decadence mixed in with a touch of today's gritty urban realism.

'I grew up in the country, in North Rhine-Westphalia, Germany, but I soon realized that the country wasn't the right place for me to be. I moved as soon as I could to Berlin to study fashion design. I had always been interested in fashion; because I couldn't get the clothes I wanted, I started making them for myself.

'During my studies, I did an internship in London, which was a great experience. I worked for a small company that supplied fast-fashion retailers like Topshop. There they designed and made the patterns, sending things to India and back very quickly. It was hard work. I had to learn all the parts of the business, but I learned a lot about the fashion industry that I wouldn't have got to know about in Germany. In fact, Topshop was one of my first customers for fishbelly, so I knew how the system worked.

'I had a very original, shocking idea for my graduation diploma called "Latex – a material between fetish and fashion". The latex project led to me looking at lingerie, as what I was doing was somewhere between fashion and underwear. So while I was still a student, I had a lot of press in magazines and also on television and radio.'

THE INSPIRATION FOR FISHBELLY
❧

'It came from the theme of my diploma: being free and wild but always fashionable. fishbelly is a name I picked up during my time in London and now it is a kind of personal expression for me, reminding me of my time in London.

'I realized that there was a market in Berlin and Germany for fashionable lingerie. I opened my first shop directly after college in 1996 and created my own lingerie line in 2002. But first of all the label was famous for being a trendy lingerie shop, selling brands such as Dolce & Gabbana and Blumarine.'

THE BERLIN INFLUENCE
❧

'At the moment Berlin is a very exciting city to live in. People come here from everywhere, especially artists. There is a lot of vibrant energy around. The design here is rather grounded, a bit rough – not so chi-chi.'

THE BOUTIQUE
❧

'The boutique is in the trendy Mitte neighbourhood. I like a relaxed, friendly atmosphere where everybody feels at home. I wanted a mix of styles; I had some rougher metal pieces made for me by a furniture designer friend of mine and I mixed it with my version of Parisian style. The wallpaper designs are Laura Ashley, and in the Turkish market I found a carpet to match them – a total mix!'

LEFT TO RIGHT:

Violet Femme, *Naughty Winter* and *Marlene*, Autumn/Winter 2007/08, photographed at the Askanischer Hof Hotel, Berlin, famous for its 1930s faded luxury

THE INSPIRATIONS FOR THE DESIGNS

'I try to get the zeitgeist, the feeling/quintessence of fashion, music, desires, visions and wishes. It's also whatever comes into my mind. For example, I have pieces influenced by Samantha from *Sex and the City* or influenced by a pin-up style or burlesque theme.'

THE DESIGN PROCESS

'I start with the fabrics; they need to make me dream and if I like them I will have an idea for the design very quickly. Sometimes I use fabrics that aren't 100% traditional lingerie fabrics but because I like them I try to find a way to make them work for lingerie. We make the samples in Berlin and the production is split between Berlin, Italy and Eastern Europe.'

PAST COLLECTIONS

'My favourite pieces are the simple ones with an extra detail that makes them special, like my triangle bra; it's simple but in a fashionable way.

'I'm proud of all the naughty designs — I've made them so elegant and desirable, and in fashionable colours, that women like to buy them for themselves.'

PHOTOGRAPHY AND STYLING

'Andy Küchenmeister is the photographer I've worked with mostly; the styling is normally done by me. I like choosing atmospheric locations. For example, for Spring 2009, with photographer Christoph Musiol, I used a classic old house in an expensive area of Berlin.'

clockwise from bottom left:
Fishbelly lingerie at KaDeWe department store, Berlin;
Spring/Summer 2009; Spring/Summer 2009

'The woman wearing fishbelly is sophisticated and cosmopolitan. She is self-confident, optimistic, open-minded and loves to play with her sexuality.'

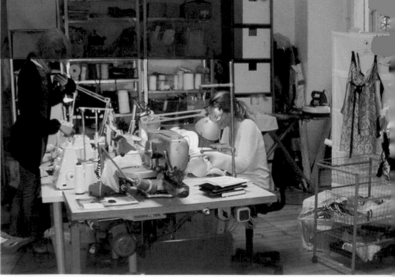

clockwise from top left:
Ice Lace, Spring/Summer 2008; fishbelly studio; fishbelly boutique (two images); fishbelly studio

Fleur of England ⚘

Fleur of England is the brainchild of Fleur Turner, who designs lingerie with a quintessentially English quality; pretty, feminine pieces with a dash of quirky humour. They are modern classics that women love for their perfect fit. The influences for her collections are often personal, linked to the events and people surrounding her life.

Fleur of England grew out of Fleur Turner's original label, Fleur T. Fleur Turner always loved drawing; her mother remembers Fleur designing corset shapes from the age of eight. Fleur even had her own fashion catwalk show while still at school. She went on to study fashion marketing at Northumbria University in the UK.

'The course is very good, because in the last year, you basically create your own brand. You have to do all the research, all the marketing, make the collection, do the graphics, cut the patterns; do absolutely everything that you would to have your own brand. I chose to do Fleur T because I knew I wanted to do lingerie design. All the collections I'd done up until then were pretty and feminine; everything featured embroidery or tulle, and my designs always pointed towards lingerie.

'I designed the collection Fleur T and also bought the .com while I was at university in 1997. I just knew it would work, from researching it; I felt really passionate about it.

'I thought it would be a mistake to start my own line straight away, so I went and worked in industry. I worked for a Marks & Spencer's lingerie supplier for a year. It was great training in understanding production. I then worked in Hong Kong for a while, saved some money and decided to work freelance and set up my own business and label in 2000; that's when Fleur T began.'

THE FLEUR OF ENGLAND WOMAN
⚘

'She really cares about fit and quality and design. All these things are important to her; she wants it all. The sexy part of it — yes, she wants that, but it's more important that it's pretty and feminine, and that it fits.'

THE INSPIRATIONS FOR THE DESIGNS
⚘

'I've always had a really strong vision of Fleur of England — it's about beautiful, stunning lingerie that is almost like a modern classic. Above all, the garment has to fit amazingly well. Fit is the most important thing. I wanted it to be feminine and pretty and beautiful. Something that if your husband or boyfriend bought for you, you would think, "Oh! How lovely, he's bought me this pretty garment, he's really thought about it!"'

THE DESIGN PROCESS
⚘

'We always start with colour and mood and then we move onto fabrics. I like to do a lot of work in sketchbooks, using fabric swatches. I sketch a collection out — it may well change from this, but these are the basic ideas. With Fleur of England it needs to work as a range, so I'll look at all the different garments and check that they are all working together.'

FAVOURITE COLLECTIONS

✥

'They are all favourites for different reasons. For example, *Tiger Lily* I love because I designed it when I was organizing my wedding, so it reminds me of happy times.

'I really love *Je ne sais Quoi*, my Autumn/Winter 2008 collection. It's very strong and I designed it when I was heavily pregnant, which I loved! I can look back at my collections and think about that time in my life and remember what I was doing when I was designing it.

'I used to have two budgies and they were the inspiration behind my collection *Tweet*. I also had a collection called *Chocolat*, because I love chocolate. I'm always inspired by the things that I love and enjoy. For example, I designed a collection inspired by my cat, Marni, called *S'il Vous Plaît*. I had to colour-match the colour of his paw to one of our silk colours.

'My Spring/Summer 2009 collection was called *Something Blue* and I colour-matched that to my little boy's jacket. I was surrounded by a lot of blue at the time, so it felt appropriate.'

FAVOURITE DESIGN

✥

'My balcony bra: the fit is really good. It's been in my collection since I started and it will never go. It's our best-seller, it has a good uplift, a really good fit, and it's the bra that I like to wear.'

LEFT TO RIGHT:

Je ne sais Quoi, Autumn/Winter 2008/09; *Black Magic* collection sketches,
Autumn/Winter 2007/08; *Fleurtatious* silk ruffle bra

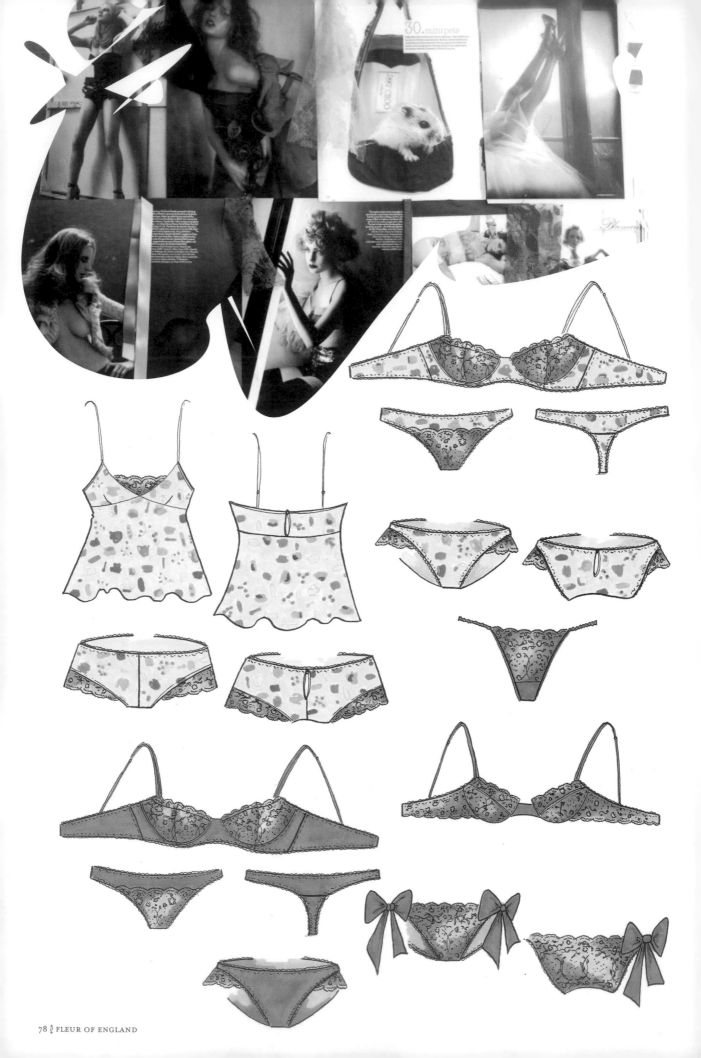

clockwise FROM TOP LEFT:

Keepsake moodboard, Autumn/Winter 2009/10;

De Mer collection drawings, Spring/Summer 2004;

Dessert moodboard, Autumn/Winter 2009/10;

Cream Tea collection sketches, Spring/Summer 2005

GÂTEZ-MOI ❧

The Japanese label Gâtez-Moi is a collaboration between founder Rinko Takaku and designer Chikage Morîta. Set around a fantasy universe that references magical flowers, cakes and French rococo, Gâtez-Moi is ultra-feminine lingerie with a quirky playfulness of spirit.

Rinko: 'I set up the label Gâtez-Moi in 2006, as I wanted to create a lingerie brand around my ideas, my world. I met Chikage Morîta in Tokyo while we were working as models for the same agency and asked her to be the designer for the brand. I've now left modelling and as well as Gâtez-Moi, I am a press and event producer and nightclub DJ.'

Spring 2008 saw the debut collection from Gâtez-Moi and Autumn 2008 the first collection of the diffusion line, Capricine. *Gâtez-moi* is French for 'spoil me' and Capricine comes from the French *capricieux*, 'capricious'.

THE INSPIRATION FOR GÂTEZ-MOI
❧

R: 'The brand concept for Gâtez-Moi is a "romantic utopia". It's lingerie that's frou-frou, delicate and makes you smile. The Autumn/Winter 2008/09 collection is entitled *Rococo Garden* and is inspired by Marie Antoinette, while the Spring/Summer 2009 collection is called *Champagne Brunch*.'

Chikage: 'I was born and grew up in Kyoto. When I was a child I loved paper craft; I was always playing with coloured paper and scissors. I was also very interested in *kamon*, Japanese family crests.

'Because Kyoto is a traditional historic city, I used to see a lot of beautiful kimonos and beautiful women wearing kimonos. So, naturally, I love the amazing colours, vibrant patterns and unexpected combinations of fabrics in the kimono. When I was modelling, I won the Kyoto Kimono Queen award for 2001.

'I wasn't necessarily interested in fashion as a child, but I always loved lace, ribbons and frills and was very interested in the details on clothes. My father is an interior designer and when I was young, I liked looking at the sample books of fabrics for curtains and so on.

'I studied dressmaking and fashion design at high school and graphic design at Kyoto City University of Arts. After university, I taught art at a high school for four years. I moved to Toyko in 2005 to become a model and also a designer in paper craft. Being a model, wearing luxury fashion, lingerie and gorgeous kimonos gave me a useful opportunity to understand fashion and lingerie. Meeting Rinko at the model agency led to me becoming the designer for Gâtez-Moi.'

THE INSPIRATIONS FOR THE DESIGNS
❧

C: 'I'm inspired by nature, such as a feeling for the seasons in Japan, the colour of the sky, sunrays from a cloud ... I love flowers, especially orchids. When I was a child, my mother taught me the names of all the flowers. I'm inspired too by the colours of sweets and fruits.

BOTH IMAGES:
Gâtez-Moi, Spring/Summer 2008

'I don't think my designs are Japanese in style, but I think that I have been influenced by the beautiful kimonos I saw when I was growing up in Kyoto, by the fabric patterns, the colours and the colour combinations. I do sometimes take inspiration from the kimono.'

THE DESIGN PROCESS

C: 'Fabrics and laces are the most important starting point for my designs. First of all, I decide on the main fabric or lace I want to use. After that, I choose the other fabrics, laces, ribbons or accessories I need to make the design as beautiful as possible. I love fabrics that have a soft touch, very lightweight fabrics, frills, polka dots and layering lace over other fabrics.

'We've also developed silhouettes that work best for a Japanese woman's body shape. All the fabrics and laces come from Japan and all the lingerie is produced in Japan too.'

PHOTOGRAPHY AND STYLING

C: 'We use different photographers and I do all the graphic design work for the styled imagery and catalogues.'

clockwise from left:
Gâtez-Moi, Spring/Summer 2008;
sketch for a lace; *Bird of Spring*
illustration by Chikage (background
detail); *Gâtez-Moi*, Autumn/Winter
2008/09; *Gâtez-Moi*, Autumn/
Winter 2008/09

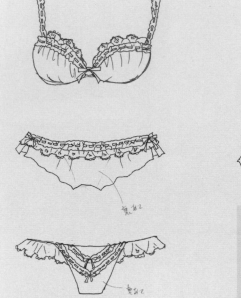

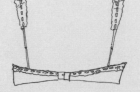

'We've developed silhouettes that work best for a Japanese woman's body shape. All the fabrics and laces come from Japan and all the lingerie is produced in Japan too.'

LEFT TO RIGHT:
Design sketches; *Gâtez-Moi*, Spring/Summer 2009; illustration by Chikage

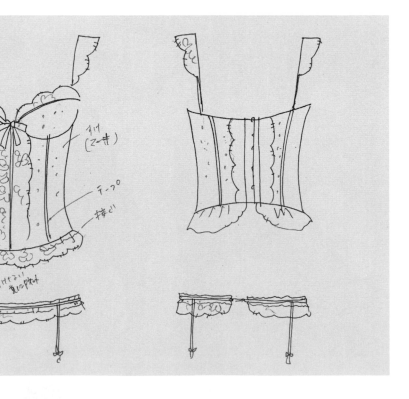

clockwise fROm above RIGHt:
Vintage-influenced design chez Gentry; *Onirique*, Autumn/Winter 2008/09;
Onirique, Autumn/Winter 2008/09

Gentry de Paris ∞

An American in Paris, Gentry Lane has explored the heart and soul of French lingerie to create pieces that evoke the spirit of 1920s bohemian Paris laced with 1930s Hollywood movie-star glamour. Her studio is set in a classic nineteenth-century Haussmann apartment, complete with a miniature pug called Napoléon.

'I've always been a Francophile; I grew up in America, taking French lessons in high school and that's where the germ started. I moved to Paris after doing my masters degree in English, and got my first job in fashion with the designer Andrew Gn. After Andrew, I worked for about ten Maisons de Couture in Paris, and after eight years I became vice-president of marketing for an upcoming designer called Frédéric Molenac.

'We wanted to expand the company and didn't know whether to start with perfume, lingerie, shoes or handbags. I met with all the head buyers of the big department stores worldwide to find out. With lingerie, they all said the same thing; "our departments are missing real French lingerie." However, we ended up doing shoes! Just as they were going to come out, our main investor pulled out her capital and the company closed. Luckily I continued to get my salary for six months and in that time and with that money I found investors to start the lingerie company that all these department stores said that they needed.

'Working with Andrew Gn, I'd learned a lot about cashmere. I had read in a biography of Coco Chanel how her first suits were made from the cashmere they used for underwear and I wondered what it was like. So I called an American lady who runs a fashion archive here in Paris and got to see and touch the Chanel suits. A friend suggested I go to Italian cashmere specialists Loro Piana, who made a special jersey just for me, based on the old Chanel design. It's super-thin, but it's durable and wears really well.

'So I launched my first collection with a range of cashmere panties, silk panties and two styles of nightgowns.'

THE GENTRY DE PARIS WOMAN
∞

'My imaginary client is a 1940s movie star. I love dressing like a movie star, too; I sleep in my gowns all the time. I love waking up fully dressed.'

THE VISION FOR GENTRY DE PARIS
∞

'It had to be like real French lingerie and made here in France. When you think of French lingerie, you think of the over-corset chemise, silk satin slips and nuisettes — bias-cut nightgowns, so that's what I made. Also, I had to keep in mind my clients and make things that were flattering for everybody's shape.'

THE INSPIRATIONS FOR THE DESIGNS
∞

'Paris flea markets — I probably have enough vintage clothes to start my own museum! I've only done one or two pieces that are reworked vintage pieces. Women's bodies were so different back then, so with vintage lingerie the proportions and sizes are completely different from today.

'I love old magazines and photos — I have a pyjama set inspired by an image of the Fitzgeralds lounging on the Riviera. Also old movies and a lot of modern prêt-à-porter; I am constantly taking pictures of people on the street.

'My real antique opium pipe, with real antique opium in it! My favourite collection of pulp fiction; these are mostly ones I got in the US. A cute stuffed mink and a "royalty shelf"; I'm obsessed with royalty and the history of Paris and London.

'I love Tallulah Bankhead and pretty much all the 1930s and 40s glamorous movie stars, like Marlene Dietrich and anyone who's luxurious. In the movie *Pal Joey* there's a scene where Rita Hayworth wakes up in the morning, her French maid comes in, pulls back the covers and she's wearing this gorgeous nightgown and then her maid brings the matching peignoir.

'The romance of artistic Paris in the 1920s is how I would like my life to be. Everybody shared models; they shared paints, they shared muses, they shared girlfriends, they shared patrons … Those jazz-age vibrations are still here in Paris; walking in Montparnasse, going to La Coupole, sitting at that bar and having a martini. It's like stepping back in time. For my first flat, I lived in the street where Kiki de Montparnasse used to live.'

FAVOURITE DESIGNS

'My bias-cut silk satin gowns, because they are really hard to do. You have to hang the silk upside down for 24 hours to make this gown. Then it's cut out and sewn together and that's what makes the line perfectly flat. It's the real French couture way. That's why my gowns are so fluid and movie-star glamorous, and cling where they should and fall where they should — on everybody, no matter what their body shape.'

FAVOURITE COLLECTIONS

'Josephine Baker was the inspiration for my first collection, *J'ai Deux Amours*, after her famous song "I Have Two Loves" — my country and Paris. The point was, I was an American in Paris, calling myself Gentry de Paris. The next one was *Madame de Pompadour's Salon* and everything was Versailles-inspired. After that came *Weekend in Monte Carlo*.

'I'd bought an old steamer trunk and inside was a pile of vintage lingerie labelled Valerianova. So we decided it had to be The Lost Wedding Trousseaux of Countess Valerianova, who fled Russia during the revolution and came to Paris and worked as a model — we make up these big background stories for everything.

'I used to be a burlesque dancer, 15 years ago in San Francisco. My burlesque name was Hermine LaMink. I've been putting on burlesque shows here in Paris since 2007. I'm now working on a club with a boudoir-style bar; a Gentry de Paris universe with a mini-boutique and pretty burlesque acts every night. I'm the only lingerie designer with her own burlesque troop, so I'm also working on a burlesque lingerie collection.'

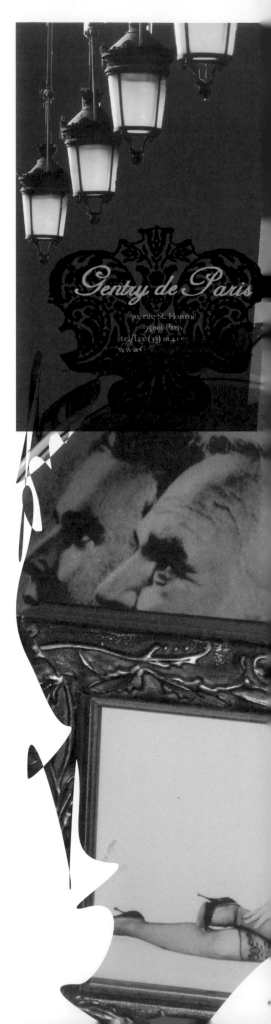

DE PARIS · SPRING SUMMER 2007
st Wedding Trousseaux
Countess Valerianova

Gentry de Paris

SUPPER CLUB &
BURLESQUE REVUE

chaque mercredi en mai

LE LUP
2 RUE SABOT ° PARIS 6e

Diner Resa Obligatoire 01.45.48.86.47
15€ Entrée · Coupe
Diner: entrée offert

Voiturier 54 rue de Rennes
~ Parking St. Germain

Info: burlesque@gentrydeparis.com

7 Mai: High Voltage Vintage Glamour
14 Mai: Cirque Coquin
21 Mai: Weimar Decadence
28 Mai: Homage à Bettie Page

21h Portes
23h Spectacle

Photo: Niel Kendall www.myspace.com/burlesquephotographer Model: Vicky Butterfly

clockwise from above:
Gentry de Paris Burlesque Revue; inspirational books and
photographs; *The Lost Wedding Trousseaux of Countess Valerianova*,
Spring/Summer 2007

Guia La Bruna ⤮

Guia La Bruna grew up around her family's lingerie business in Turin. Exploring the vintage pattern designs in the factory, combined with her art school studies in Paris, led Guia to create her heady mix of French and Italian 1950s glamour fused with a twist of the romantic modern girl.

clockwise from bottom left:
Vintage trims; *Sandman's Babe*, lurex-embroidered slip with velvet trim, Autumn/Winter 2008/09; moodboard created by Guia

'I was always interested in fashion. As my parents were in the lingerie business, I grew up surrounded by it – going around with my mother while she was buying fabrics and often using the corridors of the factory as a playground.

'My grandfather started the family business, based in Turin, in 1935, producing lingerie on a large scale. When I was a child, my parents travelled a lot, especially to Paris. I used to go with them sometimes, and I also went with them to trade shows. For me it was very exciting: the catwalk, the girls, the outfits. I still love this part of my job, when it all becomes, in a way, magical.

'As I loved Paris I wanted to move there and study art. I went to study at the École Nationale Supérieure des Arts Décoratifs, where I also learned about textile and fashion design, but I got my degree from Art Espace, which is more of a fine art-based course, studying oil painting, mosaics and sculpture, for example. I was too attracted to painting and colours to restrict myself to the textile section.

'All my technical knowledge of lingerie I learned in the factory, working for my father during college to make a little money before the summer holidays. So I started Guia La Bruna while finishing my studies. I managed to have pictures of my first collection photographed in the school by a friend of mine, who was doing a photography degree there.'

THE GUIA LA BRUNA WOMAN
⤮

'I think of a woman between 20 and 40, who is fashionable, quite romantic and feminine, in love with colours, prints, quality fabrics, with a slightly edgy taste. I guess someone like me, who loves wearing well-cut garments, in both outerwear, accessories and lingerie.'

THE INSPIRATION FOR GUIA LA BRUNA
⤮

'Vintage-style lingerie, 1950s divas mainly, all translated in luxurious fabrics. I wanted to create the lingerie set that I would love to have found in my grandmother's drawer, with a retro look but modern at the same time. I designed, for example, a white linen and lace story that reminded me of an old nightgown my grandma gave to me.'

THE INSPIRATIONS FOR THE DESIGNS
⤮

'I draw my inspiration from everything surrounding me, images that I see in an exhibition or in the street or even in magazines. I am quite confident in my personal taste when I choose fabrics. Fabrics are usually fundamental to translate the mood and they also drive me towards what I want to come out with in the next collection.'

THE DESIGN PROCESS

'I start by buying the fabrics at Première Vision in Paris; I always buy the best. Most designers draw first and then go and look for the fabrics they need, but I have never worked in that way. I always go to see what I like, what is new, what inspires me, and then think of the best way to celebrate certain colours and what shapes to put them in.

'I do a lot of research into fabrics and look for details that make my products special and unique, such as interesting ribbons. I work with companies that are involved with ready-to-wear, such as Dior or Marc Jacobs. We use expensive detailing, such as having the bras fully lined in silk.'

VINTAGE PATTERNS

'The factory kept all the information on old styles; this helped a lot for inspiration, know-how and, especially, to have an overview on what had been done before in lingerie. I started by using old patterns that I thought were still modern-looking, and just needed a couple of changes to the height or length. Some of them hardly needed changing. I even used vintage laces and trims found in the storerooms; they were still in good condition and I used them as if they were brand new. All the collection, from samples to production, is made in the family factory in Turin.'

FAVOURITE FABRICS

'My favourite fabric is silk mousseline. It has such a delicate and fluid feel and there are so many different types, including ones that are embroidered or printed with glitter. I love the way this fabric falls on the body, the soft movement it gives to all the garments. I also use cotton prints from Liberty and my other prints are either French or Italian, mainly featuring spots or tiny abstract patterns.'

FAVOURITE DESIGNS AND COLLECTIONS

'*Beauty Queen* is a favourite collection, for definite. It's an iconic style from my brand and was featured in the television series *Sex and the City*. We photographed it while I was still at college in Paris. That photo appeared in a lot of magazines at the time, so it became the very first image of Guia La Bruna.

'I have styles, such as the white linen one that I designed in the very beginning and another in a white muslin with small dots in green and pink, which I'm still wearing; it was a best-seller at that time.

'I am particularly proud of our vintage big knickers with attached suspender belt that are fully lined with pashmina from Italian cashmere experts Loro Piana. We only do this for the Autumn/Winter season. The Autumn/Winter version, *Enfant Gâté*, is in grey-green silk with matching 1950s-style bras. I love the wide black elastic — it's one of our most photographed styles.'

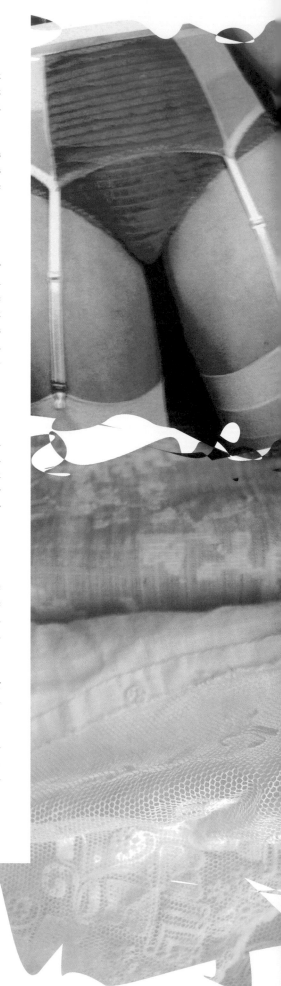

clockwise from top left:
Vintage lingerie inspiration; *Beauty Queen*, Autumn/Winter 2006/07;
Cherry collection sketches; vintage lace and embroidery inspiration

clockwise from top left:

Touch of Gold, silk mousseline with gold foil and gold sequins,
Autumn/Winter 2008/09; *Love Bow* sketch and collection image,
Autumn/Winter 2007/08; *Amore* sketch

clockwise from top left:
Collection 3 dress; silk chiffon bra; *Collection 3* dress; silk satin and chiffon

JEAN YU 〜

Jean Yu's philosophy is one of pure design. Clean graphic lines with architectural overtones lie at the origin of her lingerie, which turns the minimal into something strongly sensual. Her New York atelier dictates every stitch and seam that forms part of a Jean Yu design.

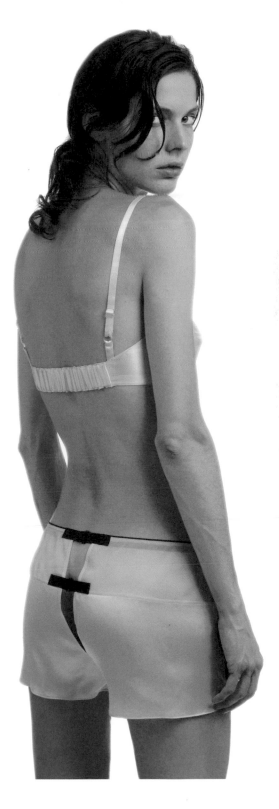

Jean Yu lingerie is designed in a controlled palette of white, black, nude and palest corsetry pink, with occasional splashes of bright colour, such as brilliant cerise or canary yellow. Contrasting elastic designed as a feature is one of her signature trademarks.

'I was born in South Korea, but grew up in South California from the age of seven. When I was eleven, I first became interested in fashion through fashion magazines, which held no language barrier for me and were something that were directly relevant. My siblings and I would visit this one big magazine stand all the time, where we negotiated a sale-and-return deal for one dollar a magazine — better than any library!

'Paris *Vogue* was a really strong influence, as was *Vogue* Italie, *Donna* and *L'Officiel*, with its sumptuous images, glossy paper and (at that time) large-size format. I also had a fondness for fine art, but my art history studies discouraged me from pursuing art as a career, as I knew how hard many struggled.

'While at high school, aged sixteen, I was already working in a highly glamorous fashion boutique in Beverly Hills, on Rodeo Drive. I then came to New York to study at the Fashion Institute of Technology (FIT). I found college rather a shock, as my student peers seemed less versed in fashion than I expected. My interests were in the technical side, as I had already learnt from my mother how to sew at an early age. After two semesters, I switched to professional classes in the evening, while making tons of money by day making custom pieces for rich New Yorkers.

'While at college we had a class assignment to create a line based on a single look, building three looks around its direction. My collection was partly inspired by the US designer Geoffrey Beene, using matt jersey in simple dress silhouettes, long and lean in clean graphic lines. This was in the mid-90s and it appeared fresh and different. I showed the collection to a few stores in Soho and got some orders. I contracted pattern-makers and sewers from FIT to help me and continued from there.

'When I left college, I wanted to have a proper dress shop — an idealized European dress shop. I have a fixation with the ultimate and best, and here it's a vertical operation — we make absolutely everything at the atelier, offering objects of desire — lingerie and dresses in silk chiffon cut from the same fabric and sewn by the same women, available both as ready-to-wear and made-to-measure.'

THE INSPIRATIONS FOR THE DESIGNS
〜

'Apart from my fixation with the ultimate and the best, my other fixation is with everything being beautiful, both inside and out. At the time, fashion was very much about wearing luxury on the outside, but for me, the ultimate is to have the luxury on the inside, where no one knows it's there.'

clockwise from top left:
Silk chiffon suspender belt; *Dresses* collection; Silk satin all-in-one, back and front

THE DESIGN PROCESS

'I don't design with a woman in mind — it's pure design and composition. I usually start with fabrics. I source fabrics from all around the world, using different types of fabric, from French silk chiffon and Swiss voiles to industrial cheesecloth. I like to shop in fabric stores in New York also, as I like the hunt for something that's a surprise. I have reserved stockpiles of fabrics that I'm very attached to — I have to be really sure about something before I cut into it.

'I often use the selvedge in my designs. It gives a very beautiful finished edge that's ultra-light, and adds an individual personality to the fabric itself. To utilize the already finished selvedge, each piece must be cut. We employ dressmaking techniques, not the automated machinery commonly used in lingerie construction. My technicians need to be able to handle silk chiffon on the bias.

'My designs evolve rather than change. I believe that good design endures — you see this in product design and also in menswear. Menswear does not change as much as womenswear and is generally better constructed. Womenswear tends to be more poorly made, due to the dynamics of the fashion season, where looks quickly flood the market and then disappear.

THE BOUTIQUE

It's an intimate but modern space where we mix ready-to-wear with lingerie. Creating the boutique helped me to define my own signature. As a designer, I found that it was very easy for me to understand what the architect had in mind and I was the one mediating with the actual workers. I was really interested in how the construction of the boutique would be realized — for me, construction is an integral part of the design.'

'The white short design that's on the homepage of my website explains visually my approach to design. It's architectural — pure composition.'

clockwise from far left:
Silk satin and chiffon; silk chiffon panty; silk chiffon slip and panty;
silk chiffon suspender belt; silk chiffon panty; silk satin and chiffon bra and panty

clockwise from left:
Autumn/Winter 2005/06; Kyuis invitation card Spring/
Summer 2009; Kyuis invitation card; Autumn/Winter
2006/07

Kyuis ❧

Kyuis is a lingerie label for the fashionable Tokyo girl about town. Founder Yuki Seo and designer Akemi Kanda create lingerie pieces that play on a Victorian innocence of lace and roses, whilst a darker, more erotic undercurrent brings us into the modern world.

Yuki: 'My mother was a very important nightwear and lingerie designer in the 1970s and 80s. It was a revolution – she changed the look of nightwear and lingerie in Japan, creating beautifully designed nightwear for women. She was very successful; her brand was very popular and it still continues today. When I was a child, my mother's brand was quite small, so I grew up in the design studio. While she worked, I played with the fabric, lace, ribbons, nightwear and dressmaking tools.'

Akemi: 'My mother was a dressmaker and worked from home. When I was a child, I loved sitting next to my mother, making dresses for my dolls. I also helped her with her dressmaking. She would make beautiful clothes for me and she taught me the important skills of fashion and dressmaking.'

Y: 'We both grew up in the city of Okayama and then we both studied at Bunka Fashion College in Tokyo. I graduated in fashion marketing and distribution and Akemi graduated in fashion design.'

Y: 'Kyuis started in 2003. I wanted to make lingerie that was girly and fashion-conscious, but also had a good fit and was styled for Japanese women. I asked Akemi to become the designer, as I knew she was really creative and talented.'

THE KYUIS WOMAN
❧

Y: 'We imagine the Kyuis woman as a woman with personality, who has her own style and enjoys fashion in her own individual way.'

KYUIS: THE NAME AND THE LABEL
❧

Y: 'The name Kyuis doesn't mean anything; we just liked the sound the word makes. Kyuis is sold in fashion boutiques, not lingerie shops, because it's a desirable fashion product, not basic underwear. We sell to well-known Japanese fashion boutique chains, such as Opaque, Jewel Changes and aquagirl.'

THE INSPIRATIONS FOR THE DESIGNS
❧

A: 'I love visiting antique markets. I'm inspired by vintage laces, embroideries and old-fashioned corsages, and by vintage porcelain and glass. I have a large vintage collection at home and I always visit antique markets when I visit Europe. Our favourite image is a shot of a camisole and short from Autumn/Winter 2004/05.'

THE DESIGN PROCESS
❧

A: 'We select the fabrics first and then discuss the new collection between us. After that, I create the sketches, make the patterns and create the sample

garments. But it depends on the style; sometimes the process is different.

'We use fabrics that are both soft and comfortable to wear and are also practical, as they are all washable. We are always continuing our research into the best-fitting patterns for Japanese women. Of course, the look should be lovely and delicate, fairy-like, cutting-edge, trendy and a little bit erotic.

'We regularly visit the trade fairs in Europe to see fabrics and laces. However, most of our fabrics and trims are from Japan, with only a small percentage coming from Europe. All our garments are made in Japan.'

FAVOURITE COLLECTIONS AND DESIGNS

Y+A: 'The Kyuis lingerie label has two sides to its character, such as sweet contrasting with erotic, luxury with popular culture, feminine with masculine, hard with soft, bright colours with dark colours, black with white.'

ACCESSORIES

Y: 'We were using such lovely fabrics for the lingerie that I thought if we made some small accessories, such as cosmetic bags, they would look really cute! They have been extremely popular.'

clockwise from far left.
Autumn/Winter 2006/07; textile inspiration; Autumn/
Winter 2006/07; vintage porcelain inspiration; Autumn/
Winter 2006/07.

'We love polka dots, leopard prints and decorative corsages. Popular pieces in the collection include unwired triangle bras, camisoles to wear as outerwear and short slip dresses.'

The Lake & Stars ❧

The Lake & Stars designers Nikki Dekker and Maayan Zilberman are dedicated to creating a lingerie label with a ready-to-wear fashion aesthetic. Both enjoy the challenge of working within the structural and functional limitations of lingerie to create designs that go beyond the conventional opposites of boudoir/functional lingerie.

Make Up Room bralette and bikini, cotton blend silk charmeuse with cotton ribbon detailing, Spring/Summer 2008; *Genius* bralette detail, stretch silk with herringbone trim, Autumn/Winter 2008

Nikki: 'We met here in New York in 2004. A mutual friend had been trying to figure out how to get us together ever since finding out he knew two lingerie designers. We hit it off instantly.'

Nikki Dekker grew up on a farm in rural North Dakota, creating her own glamour with paper dolls by the age of five. Nikki studied fashion at Minnesota, fell by chance into a job designing lingerie for Target and found, to her surprise, that it was more interesting to design than ready-to-wear.

Maayan Zilberman grew up in Vancouver and moved to New York on her own as a teenager. Maayan studied at the city's School of Visual Arts and continued to pursue art for some time before moving into fashion and then lingerie.

Maayan: 'We were both committed from the beginning to realizing our vision. We only wanted to produce a line if it would function within a designer wardrobe, as at the time one could only choose between strictly "boudoir" or "functional" lingerie and ultimately high-end or low-end. This would have to be a line that would be friendly and inclusive.'

THE LAKE & STARS NAME
❧

N: 'We found it in a Victorian novel, used as a euphemism for "great in bed", as in "she was the lake and stars". It sounds ethereal but is actually quite dirty. We thought it was perfect for the line.'

THE LAKE & STARS WOMAN
❧

M: 'A woman who will interpret our garments in her own way and style them to coordinate with the rest of her wardrobe, not as a costume. It's less about age and tax bracket, more about a state of mind and a modern attitude towards sensuality.'

THE INSPIRATIONS FOR THE DESIGNS
❧

N: 'We're really interested in opposing dichotomies — menswear vs. ultra-femininity, black-tie vs. casual sportswear, natural fibres vs. synthetic, hard detailing on soft fabrics, graphic modern shapes with antique trimmings — and what the combination of these two ends of a spectrum might look like.'

M: 'We like the ideas to remain inherent in the attitude towards the clothes, how they're worn, and how a woman will feel about herself in them. Our inspiration lies in the bigger picture, where our collections will reflect the attitudes of our customer and offer her what she really wants to wear.'

THE DESIGN PROCESS

N: 'We usually start by spending a couple of weeks alone, each researching whatever is interesting to us that season. We sketch, swatch fabrics, make colour collages, collect photographs and then come together and lay it all out. From there we fill in the blanks with combinations of details, move shapes around, and so on. There's always a lot of revision but the main themes stay the same.'

THE FABRICS AND TRIMS

M: 'A lot of our trims come from antique dealers we've encountered. Often finding a little charm or button will inform the rest of the collection. It feels special to include some personal history on a garment that someone will wear against their body.'

N: 'We try to keep fabrics/trims in the US when we can, but we find that our favourites have been from Europe, specifically France and Spain. All our garments are currently made here in New York. We want to keep a close eye on things and we're happy to keep things in the US when possible.'

THE COLLECTIONS

M: 'When we first sat at the drawing table, we had a clear idea of what materials we preferred and what features needed to be present. As we grew, the minimalist attitude we started with got layered with non-traditional references. Because we had laid out the groundwork, there was now more room to explore motif.

'My favourite example is the progression of the *We're On Break* styles from Autumn 2007/Spring 2008. In its first incarnation, in a mix of cotton/modal jersey and silk satin, it was opaque and sporty. In Spring/Summer 2009, we revisited this look in layers of silk chiffon with alternating layers of ballet tulle and trompe l'oeil suspenders. It's as though we took it through an X-ray machine, whispered in its ear and dusted it with icing sugar. It's ethereal and romantic, though strong and assertive … and highly sexual.'

FAVOURITE DESIGNS

N: 'The *We're On Break* romper is something I'm really proud of, as it really caught on and took its place in history in the *Sex and the City* movie. In general, the romper shape has been something we've really made our own. We've done a version of this shape for the last three seasons in almost every imaginable fabric and colour and it continues to remain new and interesting.'

M: 'One of the styles I'm most proud of resurrecting is the high-waisted brief. In our first season we featured it with attached garters and masculine trimmings. We've since offered it in several colours and fabrications. For Autumn 2008 we created a video project featuring dancers from New York City Ballet to present the collection; it was shot by a close friend, Matt Sundin, who has gone on to do commissioned films for us. With the ballerinas, we wanted to show them loosened up, without their hair pulled tight or constrained by tutus and corsets. It was much sexier to see the expressions on their faces and how they interacted with one another when not performing. That's what made the garments come alive.'

clockwise from top left:
Genius bralette and g-string, stretch silk with herringbone trim (left) and *Genius* romper, organic cotton jersey with cotton silk inserts (right), Autumn/Winter 2008; *Truce* romper, Spring/Summer 2009; *Love Triangle* bralette (detail), Autumn/Winter 2008

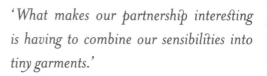

'*What makes our partnership interesting is having to combine our sensibilities into tiny garments.*'

clockwise from top left:

No Pressure bra and garter-brief, micromesh with metallic lace appliqué, Spring/Summer 2008; design inspiration, Spring/Summer 2007; *Divorcee* bralette and boyshort, woven microfibre with silk drawstrings and flying fish tassels, Spring/Summer 2007; *We're On Break* romper, Spring/Summer 2008; *Truce* romper sketch, Spring/Summer 2009

Lala Rose ⌁

Stephanie Abidjaoudi is the designer behind Lala Rose, a lingerie label based in Beirut that shines out with its vibrant, colourful silks in hot pink, yellow and turquoise. Creating couture pieces for her private clients allows Stephanie to indulge her passion for serious luxury.

'I was born in the city of Abidjan, Ivory Coast. I enjoyed a happy childhood there, in Africa, a place of treasures and discoveries. When I was nine, we moved to Beirut, my parents' home city, as my beloved grandfather was unwell, so I grew up in the Lebanon.

'From an early age I was interested in fashion and design. I drew my first collection of clothes when I was thirteen, and at sixteen I had my first brand name — French Girl. It was ready-to-wear clothing and the collection was distributed in the best shopping malls in Beirut.

'I took a diploma in interior design at USEK University in Beirut. After that, I enrolled in the Joseph Sassine fashion school, also in Beirut. I then decided to study in France, because I wanted to be successful. I discovered that fashion changed very quickly there, especially in terms of colours, styles and fabrics. I studied for four years in Paris. I went to ESMOD fashion school and I also took courses in the history of art at the École du Louvre.

'The idea for the label started in 2003. It was worth the trip to the Seychelles, where I stayed and designed my first collection. With this collection I received my first order from the Paris department store Galeries Lafayette.

'The name for the label came from a big wedding I went to in Marrakech the same year, where I kept being called Lala Stephanie — *lala* or *lalla* is a Moroccan title for a noble lady or princess, and because pink is one of my favourite colours for women's fashion (*rose* is French for "pink") I came up with the name Lala Rose — "pink princess".'

Lala Rose is sold in selective upmarket boutiques and department stores worldwide. Stephanie also has private couture clients, including Middle Eastern royalty; she was chosen to design the wedding trousseau for Saudi King Abdullah's granddaughter.

THE LALA ROSE WOMAN
⌁

'She must be chic, sensual, glamorous, active, attractive and seductive. I think that it's beautiful when a woman lets her intimate apparel reflect her personality. It's gorgeous and sensual to see a glimpse of a fine and luxurious lingerie bra through her blouse. I also believe that colourful lingerie gives out energy and positive effects.'

THE INSPIRATIONS FOR THE DESIGNS
⌁

'Every collection has a special theme, such as *Pin-Up*, *Marie Antoinette*, *Jackie Onassis*, *Disco* and *Miss Monroe*, which is a tribute to Marilyn Monroe. My latest collection is based on Indian style. During the short period I have to prepare a collection, it is the women I know or see at that time who inspire me for my next theme — their different styles, the way they wear things, their mindset,

CLOCKWISE FROM TOP LEFT:
Design sketches; *Merveille* nightdress and gown, silk satin and lace, Spring/Summer 2007, Spring/Summer 2008; *Princesse* nightdress, spot tulle, Spring/Summer 2007

their conversations. I join all of these together, trying to work on a theme that suits all kinds of today's women.

'I start by first choosing the theme. Then come the sketches, the fabrics I want to use, the laces and accessories. I then meet with my team to explain the right look for the collection and discuss patterns and production.'

FAVOURITE FABRICS

'My favourite fabrics are silk satin and fine French laces; silk mousseline and printed silks also inspire me. All our fabrics and laces come from France, Italy and Spain. All the samples and the collections are made in our own factory in the Lebanon.'

PRIVATE COUTURE CLIENTS

'I prefer to work on made-to-measure with private clients, as it fires up my inspiration for the different styles and different mindsets of the women I work with. I would characterize my private clients as charismatic, sensual, cultured, glamorous, elegant, modern and pure.'

PHOTOGRAPHY AND STYLING

'I do the styling for my photographs. With my website I want to create a relaxing, soft mood for women to discover the Lala Rose world.'

TOP SOPHIA

SHORT SOPHIA

SG. MONROE

CULOTTE MONROE

SG. AYA

CULOTTE AYA

NUISETTE ROMY

CULOTTE ANGELINA

ROBE DE CHAMBRE MERVEILLE

Lee Klabin ᕫ

London-based designer Lee Klabin has taken the corset to a higher fashion level with her made-to-measure pieces that are decorative, luxurious and dramatic. Her Notting Hill boutique Blue Poppy Couture showcases her collections, the star attraction being her curvaceous corsets.

'I've loved fashion ever since I was very young, when my father used to take me everywhere shopping with him. After growing up in various countries, I went to study at the London College of Fashion on a degree course called Product Design and Development for the Fashion Industry, which covers the business side as well as design.

'I was already interested in corsets and I started the degree hoping that there was a corset module. The module was offered in the second year, and I engrossed myself in it so much that I got a first! We really learned how to make a corset properly; how to make the patterns, how many sizes smaller it has to be than the body. I remember that, in my over-eagerness, I was the first to finish my corset, so the lecturer decided I should be the first to try it on. When she pulled the laces, it was only then that I realized what a corset can do.

'I pretty much set up my company during my second year at university. I was working from my flat, making individual pieces for family and friends. As soon as I graduated I started working full-time.'

THE APPEAL OF THE CORSET
ᕫ

'When you walk in a corset, a different attitude comes out, almost like an alter ego. Although you are the one strapped in, you feel much more in control and dominant. It is quite a strange psychological sensation — a play on femininity and seduction. You can't explain to someone what it is like to be in a corset — they have to try it, as it brings out something different in everyone.'

THE INSPIRATIONS FOR THE DESIGNS
ᕫ

'There is something about flowers in particular that are very feminine and very seductive at the same time. They are feminine in a naïve way, but seductive in a more erotic way, especially orchids, for example, which we used in our Spring/Summer 2008 collection. The peony is also a favourite; it has a multi-layered seductive quality with an initial purity that is just as disarming. If it's not a flower, it has to be something organic. I always try to contrast it with an urban and modern element.

'Normally colours come first. I have one colour in mind and that brings a few other colours into vision. Then comes the scrapbook of images that you collect and pick up. But the final deciding point is the flow of a garment or its shape and fit.'

MAKING THE CORSETS
ᕫ

'Everything is done in our studio. The base of the corset is obviously constructed by a machinist, as it has to be quite sturdy. Then there are three, or sometimes four, layers depending on the detail of the corset. All the finishing, like the quilting of the lining, is done by hand.

left to right:
Hunter and the Hunted, gold lamé wasp,
Autumn/Winter 2008/09; Lee Klabin moodboard

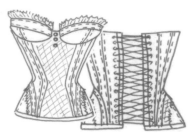

clockwise from top left:

Au Pont Neuf, Autumn/Winter 2007/08, ruffled hourglass
corset in silk chiffon, inspired by Paris's *Ancien Régime*;
corset sketches, Autumn/Winter 2008/09; the designer
Lee Klabin; *Hunter and the Hunted*, coco pearl corset, black
duchesse satin with black lace overlay, dusty rose feathers
and gunmetal pearls, Autumn/Winter 2008/09;
Apron Dress, Autumn/Winter 2007/08

'The time it takes to make a corset depends on the design. A really simple one is about a week, purely because we make it to a customer's own measurements, and the pattern cutter has to measure them – from the bust size, to the length from the underarm to the waist, from the waist to the hip – every single measurement, as it needs to fit absolutely perfectly.

'Once the patterns are done, the seamstress makes up a toile, the customer tries it on, and any alterations are made. This process sometimes takes longer than the actual construction of the corset. A seamstress can finish a simple basic corset in two days. But more decorative pieces, like the full feather ones, take two and a half to three weeks, as every feather needs to be stitched in place securely in about three to four places.'

FAVOURITE PIECES

'When I'm designing a collection, the couture corset pieces are usually the first that pop into my head and then the rest will be filtered down from that. The corset is the cherished piece – it epitomizes everything. It is the theme and inspiration of that season.

'When we launched the label, we had one corset in cream-coloured capiz shells; the shells were specially made for us in the Philippines. We made it purely as a decorative piece; it was very expensive and it took a long time to make and we never expected to sell it – but we did. It's fantastic when someone engages with that one piece that expresses everything they feel, loving it so much that they want to take it home. There is no bigger compliment you could wish for!'

Underlying corset shapes.

* a collection of very old traditional corset shapes.

* Neutral cream colours
* quite natural fabrics have a very feminine effect.

Very small waist on this corset which looks to be designed for wearing underneath.

clockwise from top left:
Corset sketches, Autumn/Winter 2008/09; corset toile; *Au Pont Neuf*, Autumn/Winter 2007/08; Sarah Jessica Parker in *Midnight Moth*; the design process

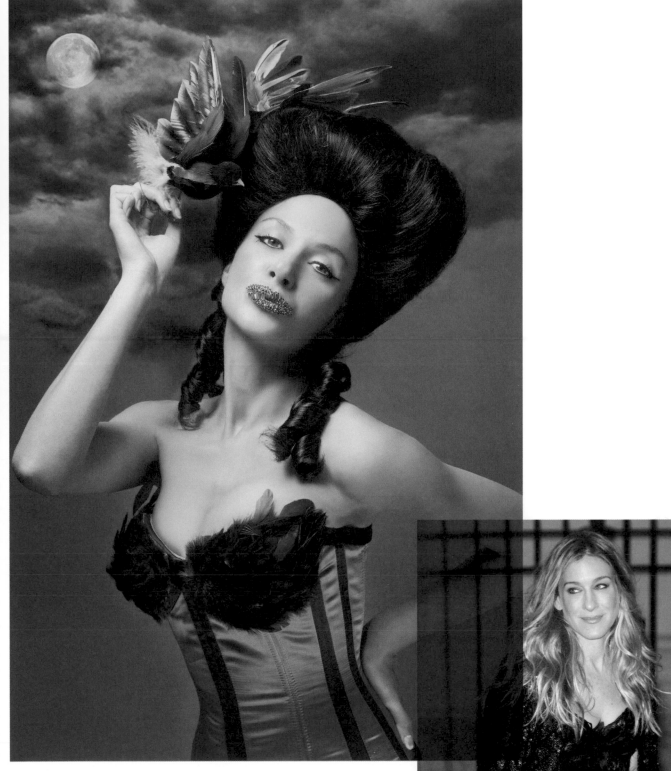

'For a small beginning label, it was such a pleasure to see such
a quick celebrity response to our designs and products.'

Louise Feuillère ⤫

Louise Feuillère creates both made-to-measure and diffusion collections of corsetry and lingerie from her atelier and boutique in the artisan 17th arrondissement of Paris. In 2007 Louise was given the prestigious Best Craftspeople of France (Les Meilleurs Ouvriers de France) award for her techniques and skill in corsetry.

'From my childhood in Boulogne, I had an interest in couture. My maternal grandmother did a lot of crochet and my paternal grandparents were involved in couture; they made shoes in Paris.

'I studied history of art at the Sorbonne and then design at ESMOD fashion school in Paris, specializing in lingerie/jersey in the final year. I learned a little about corsets there, but it was afterwards that I learned my craft while working, a lot of the time by myself. For a year I worked making orthopaedic corsets, which teaches you a lot about the geometry of the body.

'I also worked for other designers, because it was important for me to master pattern-cutting and technical skills. I worked on swimwear too, at a company that designed swimsuits for design houses, such as Chanel and Hermès. I then decided to work under my own name, with boutiques and also private clients who came to my home.'

THE ATELIER AND BOUTIQUE
⤫

'I've been here since 2002. I was originally looking just for an atelier, but this space came up in the 17th arrondissement. It's like working in a village; artisans in fashion and luxury really do live and work here still.

'I prefer to sell directly to both my private and diffusion customers from the atelier and to stay small; 100% of the lingerie is made here. It works very well having the atelier and the shop together. The clients like coming here and I have customers from everywhere, including Canada and the US.

'The first time I put a bra in the window, it made me feel very proud. I was astonished by women's reactions to the design; it was very original. Women would stop, take a little step back, turn round and look — at something of mine.'

THE INSPIRATIONS FOR THE DESIGNS
⤫

'In a fashion studio you need inspiration to design, but I've already passed the drawing stage, because I've already got the fabric and so I can design in any way I like. It starts from finding fabrics that you love. For example, I've bought a beautiful lace that I've started working with. I don't know where the design is going, but that's how I work. I work on the mannequin and I don't have any sketches. And then afterwards, I draw the designs out on paper!

'My antennæ and my moods are also involved. I'm inspired by everything I see in the world around me. I have a lot of books on the eighteenth and nineteenth centuries. I like to visit exhibitions, archives and museums, especially for paintings. I go to lots of secondhand shops and flea markets in Paris, where I might buy small pieces of lace or ribbons.'

clockwise from top left:
The boutique interior; silk and lace basque; made-to-measure.

VARGAS PIN-UPS

'The Vargas images are superb, they're something that inspire me, because they are a little flirtatious, a whole world of seduction. The Vargas woman isn't a real woman; it's an idea — I've never met a woman with a figure like a Vargas woman. Vargas liked to play with transparent fabrics and it's a theme that I also have in my work. People say I have a talent for designs that use transparency, as I adore working contrasting fabrics together.'

FAVOURITE FABRICS

'I work mostly with French suppliers for laces and fabrics; it's important to me, because of keeping jobs in France. I adore lace and cotton, but I don't like silk because it's not practical for everyday life. Even if you buy a really fine quality, it's never as perfect as jersey or a synthetic fabric. Silk doesn't wash well. The silks from after the war, woven in the 1940s and 50s, were actually washable. There's still some old stock around; I've made designs from it.'

MADE-TO-MEASURE

'It's my made-to-measure work that I'm most proud of. To dress a woman in lingerie or to sculpt the body of a woman is a very difficult skill that demands workmanship of a very high quality — aesthetic, technical, good taste, customer service, listening, intuition … today's professionalism is to anticipate clients' requests.

'I've also created made-to-measure corsets inspired by images from nineteenth-century books and illustrations. I like to take these corsetry details and use them on new models, such as a push-up-style bra.

'In made-to-measure there's no pre-considered design silhouette; it's a different way of working, especially for bras. For example, there's a special way of sewing the cups into the bra that isn't done in industry. When I make these luxury pieces, I work with millimetre measurements and it shows in a beautiful bust shape, because these designs have really come from artisan work.

'My favourite designs are those I've yet to design. As soon as a design is finalized, I'm not interested in it any more; the work is done and I can have fun playing with another idea.'

LES MEILLEURS OUVRIERS DE FRANCE (MOF) AWARD

'MOF is an organization that gives awards to the best craftspeople of France. The awards occur every three years, and there hadn't been an MOF awarded in lingerie since 1979. I registered and had to choose a category — I chose corsetry, and submitted a waspie corset inspired by the 1950s.

'I had to make the design using certain techniques, proving my *savoir faire* and skill. The award is judged anonymously. I received a letter to say I had passed. There was a medal award ceremony at the Sorbonne, and in January 2008 we were invited to the Élysée Palace for a presentation with President Nicolas Sarkozy. MOF helps you to become better known, as it holds a lot of exhibitions throughout France. You meet a lot of people working in the MOF — it's like a "luxury" family group.'

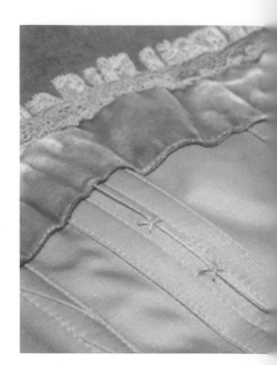

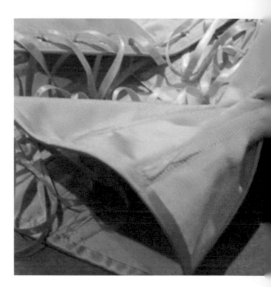

clockwise from top left:
Detailing on made-to-measure corset inspired by nineteenth-century designs; inspiration; sheer corset; detailing on made-to-measure corset inspired by nineteenth-century designs

clockwise from below left:
Attaching lace to a robe; bra inspired by nineteenth-century
corsetry; designing directly onto the mannequin; design sketches

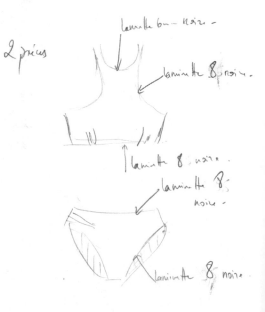

LEFT TO RIGHT:
Limited edition *Hidden Treasure Bra* in
sparkling jersey, eyelash lace, black
satin, detachable pearl jewellery,
Autumn/Winter 2008/09; sketches;
Magic Bum Girdle with hidden power
panels to lift the bottom, flatten
the tummy and slightly cinch the
waist, plus *Front Cinch Bra*, Fresh
Foundations, Spring/Summer 2009

Made by Niki ❧

Niki McMorrough is the designer behind the lingerie label Made by Niki. From ultra-exclusive numbered items to glamorous shapewear, Niki has a clear focus on what the modern woman wants from her lingerie — and she creates it. These innovative pieces originate from the Made by Niki studio in the heart of the English countryside.

'After school, I took a degree in European Studies and started on a successful career in media and promotion in London. While working and living in Soho, I used to spend a lot of my lunchtimes and wages collecting lingerie (and shoes!) from Agent Provocateur, Fenwick, Selfridges and Liberty. I thought it was a "normal" interest, but my friends now tell me I was verging on the obsessed.

'I would dream of having my own business making something personal, luxurious and beautiful. I had a need to make a real product — a product that you could touch and feel. My background was in media and, with everything you do in the media, the minute it's finished, it's gone. I wanted to create something and it had to be something really beautiful. I used my free time to do short courses at the London College of Fashion (Setting Up A Fashion Business and Introduction to Lingerie) that gave me an insight into the business and product. I also took courses in screenprinting and textiles.

'I knew about this amazing Contour Fashion degree at De Montfort University in Leicester. It's 100% focused on lingerie design and is the only degree of its kind in the world. It's very exclusive, but luckily I was accepted there in 2005. I was so excited that I gave up a job offer in Sydney for it! My fiancé (now husband and business partner) Scott Parker had to come back with me. That's how dedicated we are to this brand — we gave up everything to do this.

'As a mature student, I could fast-track the course. By the end of 2006 I was already up to my ears in Made by Niki, designing collections, exhibiting at trade shows, collating all the fabrics, wrangling with lawyers and wrestling with our website. By then, the brand was already stocked in stores such as Coco de Mer and Barneys.'

THE MADE BY NIKI WOMAN
❧

'She's a confident, sassy, busy girl-about-town who values quality, fit and fashion. Basically, that's me. I wear all my own designs and this is an important part of the development process — so I can make them feel fantastic as well as look hot. From the office to the shops to the dancefloor, they have a job to do. I even wore a Fresh Foundations wedding gown down the aisle.'

THE LIMITED EDITIONS
❧

'The limited editions were our first entry into the market and were handmade by me. Even today they are still partly made by me; I personally paint the gold number onto the garment and attach the certificate of authenticity. The concept began as an anti-globalization comment, based on the idea that people should know who their products are coming from.'

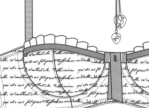

THIS PAGE:
Limited edition *Loveletter* bra in cotton printed with a handwritten love letter and detachable gold heart jewellery, Autumn/Winter 2008/09; sketch for *Loveletter* bra

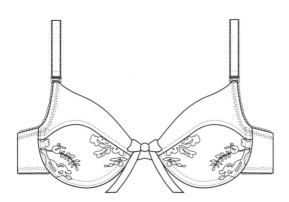

THE INSPIRATIONS FOR THE DESIGNS

'We are inspired by what's not there, not by what's already around. We search for gaps in the market and then fill them. For example, there were no brands making gorgeous, sexy shapewear, so we launched Fresh Foundations, our luxury body-shaping lingerie. It's inspired by the shape of the body and what women want and need in their wardrobes.'

THE DESIGN PROCESS

'It starts with research — either conscious or unconscious observation. Then comes a sketch, either on paper or just in my head. I will come up with shape options and then narrow it down. The fabrics and jewels are important, as they can help to communicate the idea.

'Fresh Foundations is much more shape-driven than the limited editions. The fabrics are chosen for their function and range of colour options, as we like to offer Fresh Foundations in lots of colours. Nearer to the launch date, we will review the colour, shape and style to ensure it will complement what people will be wearing that season, sometimes altering the height of the waistline or the shade and tone.'

FAVOURITE COLLECTIONS

'*Think of England*, my first collection, will always have a place in my heart. I love working with tweeds and traditional suiting fabrics. It was very special as I personally made 100% of the bras and corsets, from start to finish. There were only 20 of each colourway worldwide.

'The *Rosary* collection was also very special, as I hand-dyed all the fabrics myself and made all the jewellery using Swarovski pendants and rosary beads. It caused a lot of discussion among people involved in the world of fashion, religion and politics because of its unique blend of purity and naughtiness. We had 666 complaints on the day we launched it. It's very popular as a bridal gift, and with men buying for lovers.'

THIS PAGE:
Shape Shorts in black stretch satin and French gold lace 'flatten and flatter' with side-fastening zip, plus *Multiway Plunge Bra*, Fresh Foundations, Autumn/Winter 2008/09; sketch for *Multiway Plunge Bra*

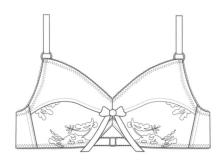

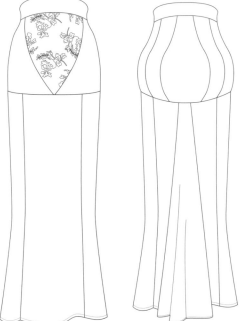

clockwise from top left:

Sketches of *Wireless Front-Cinch Bra*, which offers support with no underwires, in stretch satin and lace; worn with co-ordinating *Suspender Skirt* with hidden sculpting support, Fresh Foundations, Autumn/Winter 2008/09; Fresh Foundations, Spring/Summer 2009; *Think of England*, Autumn/Winter 2006/07; *Rosary*, Autumn/Winter 2006/07

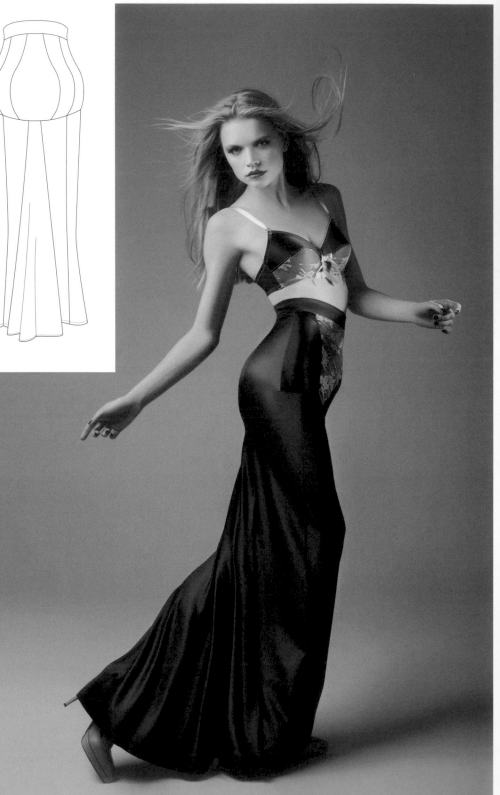

Made by Niki

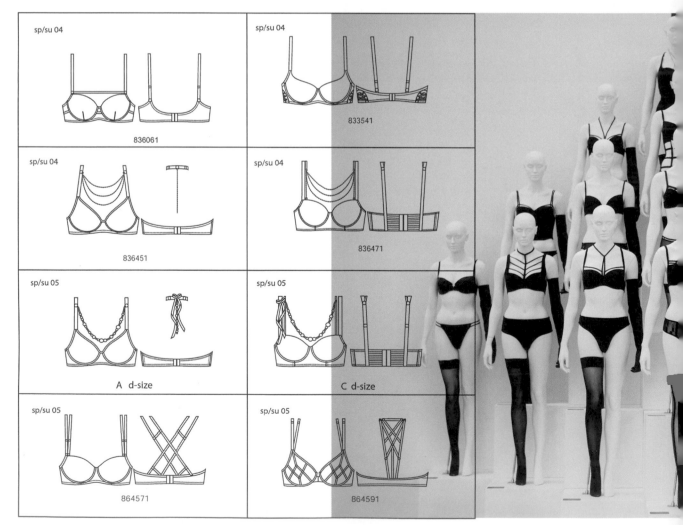

Marlies Dekkers ⤐

Dutch designer Marlies Dekkers has never compromised on her vision of what lingerie should mean to women. Her provocative pieces challenge both traditional feminism and the classic cliché of lingerie worn to please men, by advocating a new sensuality based on women's freedom to enjoy lingerie on their own terms.

clockwise from top left:
Secret Spider, Spring/Summer 2004; Marlies Dekkers exhibition, Kunsthal Rotterdam 2008; *Secret Spider* sketches, Spring/Summer 2004

'My mother always had a sewing machine up on the kitchen table, making clothes for me and my sister, as we didn't have much money. Nearly every night, I would watch her make patterns and sew, and from the age of around five or six I would copy – cutting out my own designs and sewing. Even when I was very young I was already fascinated by lingerie. I think it was because it was so beautiful and so sexy and also it was a big mystery; a mystery I couldn't understand at the time.

'I studied fashion at Breda School of Art and from the beginning, of all the projects we did, mine became lingerie! Or they were somewhere in between – not really outerwear, not really underwear, like the *Bare Buttocks Dress* I designed for my graduate collection. My work was very conceptual and even the tutors didn't see it as lingerie. I liked to design "close to the body" fashion, so my early work already had that signature.

'When I graduated in 1991, suddenly I had a eureka moment – "It's lingerie". I started my brand in 1993, calling it Undressed by Marlies Dekkers. For me, a woman's body is always most beautiful when naked; everything that I add to it, the chances are that I will make it less beautiful. That's why I chose the name Undressed, as it forces me to work very hard to try to make it more beautiful than the undressed body.'

The brand now encompasses more than 1,000 points of sale worldwide, plus six boutiques in the Netherlands, and stores in Antwerp, Berlin, Cologne, Paris, New York and Bangkok.

THE MARLIES DEKKERS WOMAN
⤐

'"I am as beautiful, as sensual, as desirous as I believe myself to be" – this quote comes from my book *33 Propositions* [written by Marlies Dekkers in conjunction with Meghan Ferrill]. The words "I believe myself to be" are important, as we might believe we can wake up as Kate Moss and it doesn't happen! Women tend to have a different view of who they are; I try to create designs that allow women to accept themselves as they are and feel comfortable about this. I want to give them confidence and make them feel beautiful. That's my mission!'

WORKING AS A DUTCH DESIGNER
⤐

'I was invited to curate an exhibition of my work at the Kunsthal Rotterdam in 2008. I included work from De Stijl, Mondrian and Rietveld, to show that, for me, it has a real connection with the DNA of the Dutch. If you look at Marcel Wanders and Moooi or other Dutch artists, we all have elements of the same handwriting.

'For lingerie, this translates into a desire to reduce and pare down – the beauty of simplicity. I think it is also typically Dutch that I like to design around "lines". I do it with straps, whereas Rietveld, for example, used "lines" in wood to make his famous Red Blue Chair.'

THE DESIGN PROCESS

'It's an ongoing process, because we have seven collections per year. It's a way of living — collecting, looking at the world, taking photos, going to museums, reading books and so on. Take my *Sleeping Beauty* collection from Spring/Summer 2008. From the fairy story, I liked the idea of the drop of blood and all the flowers around the castle where she slept for 100 years. It's a process about the things that inspire you and you think them through. Then you start designing, working out what kind of flower it should be, reading up about flowers and their meanings. Then you can continue layering the story through the print because you've chosen a flower with a specific meaning.'

FAVOURITE COLLECTIONS

'That's like asking which of your children you love the most! All my collections are like a diary; they reflect my moods at that time. You may be more romantic or more erotic, perhaps more daring or more shy; all these different moods have a value for me — one isn't valued over another.'

FAVOURITE DESIGNS

'When I started in lingerie, the moulded seamless bra was purely functional. It's not a shape I invented, but I think I've made it fashionable and modern, and also sexier! Traditionally, we see a non-wired bra in a sheer fabric as the sexier bra, but I've made the moulded bra sexy. That's something that I'm proud of; in a moulded bra, you look five kilos slimmer, whereas a non-wired bra makes your breasts look flat as a pancake and you don't have the same beautiful figure.

'I'm also very proud that I design underwear that women want to combine with outerwear. Many women who buy my bras buy the bra first and then the outerwear, because they want to show it off. When I started in 1993, all the store buyers said, "I can't sell that, you can see the bra straps!". When I said that it was meant to be like that, they would reply, "Oh no, women want their bra to be invisible". I explained that I wanted to make them so beautiful that women would want to show them off, and the buyers didn't believe me. I'm very proud that years later I've been proved right and it is something women like to show off.'

clockwise from left:

Bare Buttocks Dress, designed in 1991, Kunsthal Rotterdam 2008; *So Dutch*, Spring/Summer 2007; *Give and Take*, Spring/Summer 2009; *Made and Adored*, Spring/Summer 2009; *Powerful Grace*, Autumn/Winter 2008

clockwise from top left:

Tropical Birds, Marlies Dekkers exhibition, Kunsthal Rotterdam 2008; Marlies discusses designs with her sister Anja, senior designer at marlies|dekkers; *Sleeping Beauty*, Spring/Summer 2008 at marlies|dekkers store, Berenstraat, Amsterdam; marlies|dekkers store, Cornelis Schutstraat, Amsterdam; *Luna Park* catwalk show, Amsterdam International Fashion Week, January 2008

LINGERIE DE LUXE

Miss Lala Presents ᑐᑐ

Miss Lala Presents lingerie features a delightful cocktail of influences, mixing 1930s Hollywood glamour with the romance of European 1950s chic and a dash of glittering crystals. Served up by Fine Rees, famous for her tiny but exquisite Primrose Hill lingerie boutique in London, the collection is story-telling retail at its best.

clockwise from top left:
Retro Parisian influences; *Rainbow*, candy pink and cream silk, Spring/Summer 2009; Covent Garden boutique; 1950s Danish fashion magazines

'I grew up in England, but my biggest inspiration came from my mother's Danish family, who came from a tiny island called Langeland. My Danish grandmother was a huge inspiration. She kept everything — the stockings she'd worn for her wedding, powder puffs she'd been given at eighteen that had never been out of their boxes.

'From fourteen I became obsessed with lingerie. I discovered the benefits of padded balcony bras and started coveting La Perla too. I had a rich friend who had a mirrored 1920s chest of drawers full of matching La Perla underwear — all colour-coordinated. That was my aim in life — drawers full of perfectly matching lingerie.

'I wanted to be an actress. I went to film school in Denmark and worked in television in Copenhagen, where I discovered a love of interiors; the shops and interiors are really beautiful — it's very cosy. I then went to UCLA theatre school in L.A. and worked as an actress. I loved the glamour of 1930s Hollywood, the beautiful hotels, shabby chic shops and story-telling lifestyle stores.

'I had an idea for a shop called Lala's Boudoir — "Lala" from Lalaland, L.A., and I loved boudoir chic. I then saw Degas' painting of a trapeze artist, *Miss Lala*, and the name came to me — Miss Lala's Boudoir!

'I came back to England aged twenty-six (as I didn't become a famous movie star). I saw a to-let sign outside this tiny old shop in Primrose Hill where I lived, and I decided to open the shop.'

MISS LALA'S BOUDOIR, PRIMROSE HILL
ᑐᑐ

'It was Hollywood glamour and pin-up girl, mixed with a Parisian influence. There was also a Danish influence from the 1930s and 40s, and from the black and white movies of that era that I'd seen in my childhood. I wanted items that I couldn't find; the big tutu skirts I'd seen in *Sex and the City* and gingham aprons with little pin-ups on them. I met lots of designers who could make things that weren't in other boutiques. It was meant to be a boudoir chic lifestyle store. But the lingerie sold well and we started to be known as a lingerie boutique, with me having a big reputation as a lingerie buyer! I'd never worked in commercial lingerie, but I bought with my heart.'

THE MISS LALA PRESENTS LINGERIE COLLECTION
ᑐᑐ

'I was buying directional pretty bras, soft cup bras, but they didn't sell well as they didn't have the fit. Through a friend I met the Stirling Group, which has great technical experience in fabrics, production and manufacturing, and we became partners. Miss Lala Presents is now sold globally. We've been successful because we have the commercial knowledge of what people want to wear. It's got to fit and it's also about comfort. Also, all the pieces are silk-lined — all these things matter.'

THE MISS LALA PRESENTS WOMAN

'She's always in my mind when I buy for the shop. I ask myself the same questions: Is it glamorous? Is it retro-inspired? Is it feminine and girly? I start my own lingerie collections the same way.

'The second factor is that, with lingerie, you never know who's going to buy what. You can think, for example, that pink gingham is for a certain age group, but you can have a fifty-year-old woman come in who adores it. Lingerie is the one place where you can really experiment. I want girls to buy it, women to buy it and mothers to buy it for their daughters. It's about making a girl feel wonderful. Maybe the girl might be single — it is flirtatious.'

THE INSPIRATIONS FOR THE DESIGNS

'It's often from an object. My first story started with a velvet dress. Christopher Cane had just done velvet, so I came out with *Velvet Goldmine* in Winter 2007. The second story came from a beautiful pillowcase embroidered with lovely flowers and the words "Be Happy" — I have a lot of Danish post-war memorabilia, such as porcelain cups and linens. Recently, we recreated in velvet flocking some old silhouette prints from the 1950s that my mother brought over from Denmark.'

FAVOURITE FABRICS AND PRINTS

'I'll never stop loving polka dots. I'm obsessed with hearts. Ginghams I just adore, and also 1950s cotton stripes; I love the colours. I like a bit of bling — I like Swarovski crystals.'

FAVOURITE DESIGNS

'My favourite from Spring 2009 is *Rainbow*. I love the little heart on the pocket, inspired by tennis girls from the 1970s. The rainbow comes from 1970s disco girls and roller blades. My boyfriend has a pair of white roller skates that I was desperate to get into a photoshoot. My *Be Happy* knickers are a key for me, and I really love the poodle bra and knickers we did for Spring 2008. I like detailing, such as the printed silk linings inside our *Be Lucky* bra cup and our silk bras with bagged-out finishes.'

COLLABORATIONS

'I love doing collaborations with the designers we sell in the shop. For example, we sold Miss Budd's accessories in the shop and we had a Miss Budd pin-up print lingerie collection for Winter 2008.'

PHOTOGRAPHY AND STYLING

'Photoshoots are part of telling a story and branding the image. It's important to me to have a girl with a womanly figure who looks slightly older, sensual, but not provocative. I collaborate with the photographer — we don't have a stylist. I prefer to use locations rather than a studio, and we normally use the home of someone we know. Each time we try and tell a story about why this girl is living in this house and why she's by herself. The last one was a story of a girl who's going out with a racing-car driver and been left in this big house by herself and is terribly bored ...'

clockwise from top left:
Les Girls, silk bra, frilled knicker and bed jacket with Peter Pan collar, Spring/Summer 2009; *Poodle* knickers, Spring/Summer 2008; *Velvet Goldmine*, Autumn/Winter 2007/08; Miss Lala Presents packaging

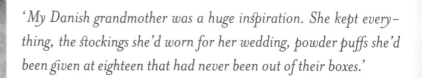

'My Danish grandmother was a huge inspiration. She kept everything, the stockings she'd worn for her wedding, powder puffs she'd
been given at eighteen that had never been out of their boxes.'

clockwise from top left:
Retro Parisian influences; 1950s Danish women's novels; *Chocolate
Box*, inspired by 1950s pleated silk fabrics, Spring/Summer 2009;
Vintage Pearls, vibrant emerald green silk with pink silk tulle trim, plus
double-faced silk kimono, Spring/Summer 2009

Nona Samimi
Boutique

ENGLAND

N De Samim ⟷

Nona De Samim's love of creating private worlds of decadence and luxury led her to develop her lingerie label, N De Samim. Nona's experience as an interior designer and stylist and love of all things French allows her to create lingerie whose inspiration ranges from sixteenth–century châteaux to ladylike tea salons.

Nona De Samim is Persian and was born in Tehran, leaving at the age of nine to come to the UK. She started her studies with a degree in fashion illustration and promotion at Epsom School of Design (now University College for the Creative Arts), and then did a masters degree in design and marketing.

'I have always been drawn to antiques, and after university I took a course at Sotheby's, falling in love with the Italian Renaissance and all periods of French interior design.'

'While freelancing for *Vogue* as a stylist, I started designing and selling interior products – screens, paintings, cushions and so on. Developing from my interest in interiors, I started to bring back treasures from the flea markets in France and Italy. I would sell everything at once-a-month parties held in my showroom and apartment, which is in one of Brighton's historic Regency squares.

'I realized that I had a talent for creating totally immersive environments; a "story-telling" retail experience. So I took my love of French culture and developed it into the world of N De Samim, designing my first collection in 2006.'

THE N DE SAMIM WOMAN
⟷

'I tend to like really sexy women such as Monica Bellucci or Claudia Cardinale. I like real women; I think that's why I've gone into lingerie. But I also think you just need an attitude to wear my lingerie, not a particular body shape; someone strong and adventurous.'

THE INSPIRATIONS FOR THE DESIGNS
⟷

'I became totally obsessed with antiques. Initially, I was drawn to the Italian Renaissance. I like religious icons. I like taking things and breaking the rules. I love all the designs from the Renaissance, for example, but then I'd add something really sexual – then it would become controversial. I then fell into French antiques. I absolutely adore everything French, including lingerie. I was constantly in the antique and flea markets in Paris.

'I like people, characters, atmospheres and smells, and I work from that rather than acting as a traditional fashion designer. It just all comes together and becomes a product. It became lingerie: I could have opened a flower shop and I would have translated it the same way.

'From fashion I'm inspired by Lanvin, vintage Dior, and I love Marni.'

THE DESIGN PROCESS
⟷

'I could start with a scene in a film, perhaps. I'm inspired by music, anything – things that are not directly linked with fashion. I like arthouse movies and I like 1960s Italy, but it could be anything.

'I get an idea, and I sketch and sketch and when it looks right, I start looking for the fabric. It's the shape and the story that matters to me. For example, I imagine a woman scrubbing the floor in Versailles, and start from there.'

THE COLLECTIONS

'My first collection was called *Sans Culottes*. The trend for thongs was at its height; girls thought it was so sexy and it really wasn't! I started reading about lingerie and the history behind it. In sixteenth-century France, which is one of the main influences behind the brand, it was considered indecent by the bourgeoisie to wear any underwear at all. Prostitutes and dancers were the only women who wore any undergarments.

'So I turned it round, saying that it is actually more decent to show more. I like breaking the rules, so I created an alternative to the thong. It has a silk front with an open-back garter, plus a detachable lead, which adds a sexual connotation, that can be worn outside the jeans for added mystery.'

FAVOURITE COLLECTIONS

'In the *L'Atelier Parisien* collection, my favourites are my *Avec des Bas* foundation knickers in powder blue canvas. They remind me of a sofa covering, very Marie Antoinette. They come with white stockings.

'I also like my *Sans Jupons* petticoats; I thought they were really feminine. I like to bring something new out of something old – you break the rules and things become modern. You can make anything sexy – I just pick something that I know and then I change it.'

clockwise from top left:
Avec des Bas foundation knickers and
stockings, *L'Atelier Parisien*; *Bas des Corps
Souffle*, Basics; fashion influences;
Sans Culottes, Autumn/Winter 2006/07

clockwise from top left:
Sans Culottes; inspiration from the colours of traditional French pâtisseries; the design process; *La Couture de Pâtisserie*, inspired by the memories and colours of nineteenth-century French pâtisseries

clockwise from below:

Louise, Chantilly lace camisole with ribbon-slotting trim; *Gina*, silk satin camisole with cotton lace;
vintage slip in ivory tulle, 1925; *Sophia* basque in Chantilly lace and silk satin

Nuits de Satin Paris ❧

Ghislaine Rayer is the force behind Nuits de Satin Paris. Starting out with a boutique specializing in vintage corsets and lingerie, Ghislaine now recreates these increasingly rare pieces for today's connoisseuse. Her knowledge of past techniques and details allow her pieces to be true to the French tradition of savoir faire.

'I've always loved lingerie. When I was young, I adored nineteenth-century literature, set in France during the Second Empire or the beginning of the Victorian era in England. My favourite novelist is Émile Zola. He wrote *Au Bonheur des Dames* ("The Ladies' Paradise"), based on the early years of Le Bon Marché in Paris. It's the story of a silk merchant who grows his business into this huge department store. It was the first time that lingerie and corsets were sold in a shop, with their own departments. The book contains lots of descriptions – Zola wrote copiously! It became my total passion – I imagined myself passing through the departments of the store. He describes fabrics and materials that I didn't know at all; he wrote a lot about lace and the making and selling of this lingerie worn by nineteenth-century women.

'From then on, I became fascinated by lingerie, especially corsets, and I started collecting pieces. I didn't start off working in lingerie. I was working as an insurer in the music industry and Johnny Hallyday was one of my clients. We often had to accompany the artists on tour and so I came to meet Johnny's cameraman, Patrice Gaulupeau. He had a passion for vintage lingerie also and suggested we opened a boutique at the Paris flea market. At the time, you could only find vintage lingerie in shops selling vintage linens.

'We opened the boutique in the Saint-Ouen flea market in 1999 and it was an immediate success. To begin with, there was only my own personal collection – there was practically nothing to sell. My first client was the lingerie designer Chantal Thomass. Gradually dealers started to bring me pieces, and I collected accessories, magazines and so on as well, and I received a lot of press worldwide.

'In 2005, we opened a boutique and showroom in the 16th arondissement. But it became more and more difficult to find vintage lingerie, especially the lingerie that I bought, which was always the best quality and had to be unworn. I felt also that a part of French heritage was disappearing and it would be better if we kept the best pieces and created a private museum with them. My clients all said what a shame and how beautiful our pieces were. So I thought, why not recreate vintage pieces from specific eras? Therefore, in January 2006, I started the Nuits de Satin Paris collection with Patrice.'

THE DESIGN PROCESS
❧

'We take several vintage pieces and use one detail from one, another detail from another — we don't design on paper. Or we take a vintage design as a base and design around it. For example, take this nineteenth-century riding corset. It's like a mini-corset, because the normal corset was too long for riding, and in the nineteenth century every well-bred woman had to wear a corset, even when she was riding a horse. So we recreated it in a slightly more modern style. It gives you a real wasp-like waist. It's expensive because it's very, very difficult to make; if the sewing is out by just one millimetre, the waspie won't work. I'm the only one who knows how to make them.'

THE FIRST DESIGNS

'At the start, we took the pieces we really liked and the pieces that you couldn't find anywhere else. For our bras, we work with Chantilly Leavers laces that are used only for haute couture, not modern lingerie laces that have stretch — I don't like stretch laces. All our laces are rigid; they are a lot finer, but a lot more expensive too!'

VINTAGE DETAILS

'There are details that are impossible to make now. Years ago, well-bred young ladies would sew their own lingerie for their marriage trousseaux. If the family was rich, they would pay seamstresses to make it — all by hand. They took an enormous amount of time, so it would be impossible to recreate that work.

'There are also techniques that are very complicated and it's difficult for us to find factories today that are capable of making certain pieces. In the average factory, the time allotted to make a basque is 15 minutes; for ours, it's two and a half hours! But our lingerie will really reshape your figure; something they knew all about in the 1950s. If a woman wears mass-market lingerie in stretch fabrics or lace, it stretches to fit, whatever the size. With ours, that's impossible. A 38 is a 38, a 40 a 40 and at the same time, it redefines your silhouette.'

FAVOURITE FABRICS

'I adore Chantilly lace, silk mousseline and silk satin, especially duchesse satin. I also use batiste; a fine cotton weave. I only really like noble, natural fabrics. All the fabrics are French, including the silk, because I believe France has a unique *savoir faire* with regard to fine-quality fabrics and laces.'

VINTAGE LINGERIE EXHIBITIONS

'We have the world's largest private collection of corsets and underwear, consisting of nearly 10,000 pieces. We organized the first exhibition ourselves in Paris in 2004; everyone said how fabulous it was. We then had other exhibitions in France and at the Salon International de la Lingerie. Now we lend pieces to museums for different exhibitions, such as the "Secrets — The Lure of Lingerie" exhibition held at the St. Gallen Textile Museum in 2008.'

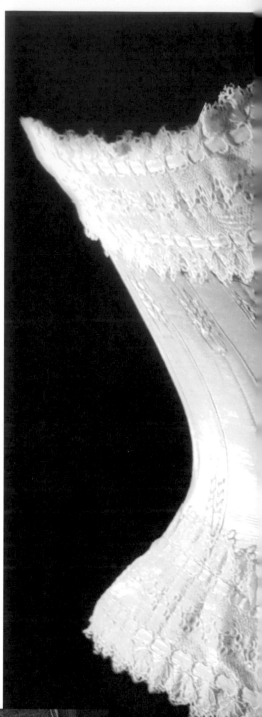

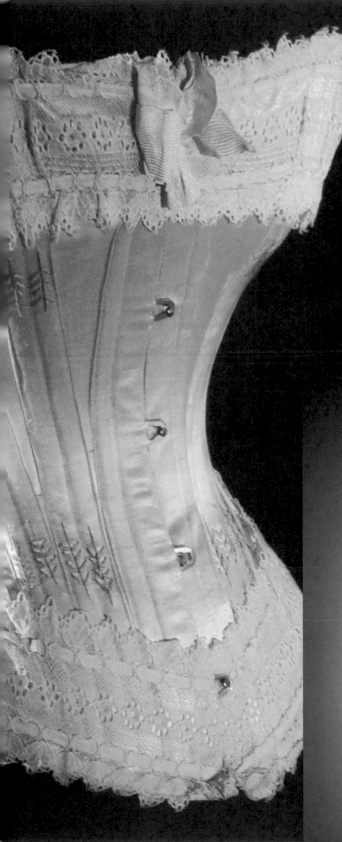

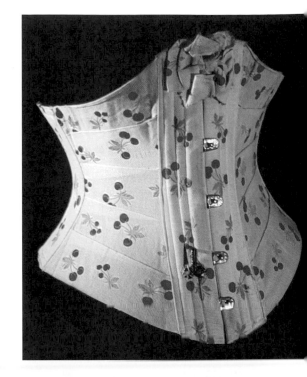

clockwise from bottom left:

Vintage eveningwear corset, 1890; silk bridal corset, 1890; riding corset created from jacquard ribbons, 1905; *Dita* waspie created from violet and black cotton ribbons, with *Dolly* babydoll

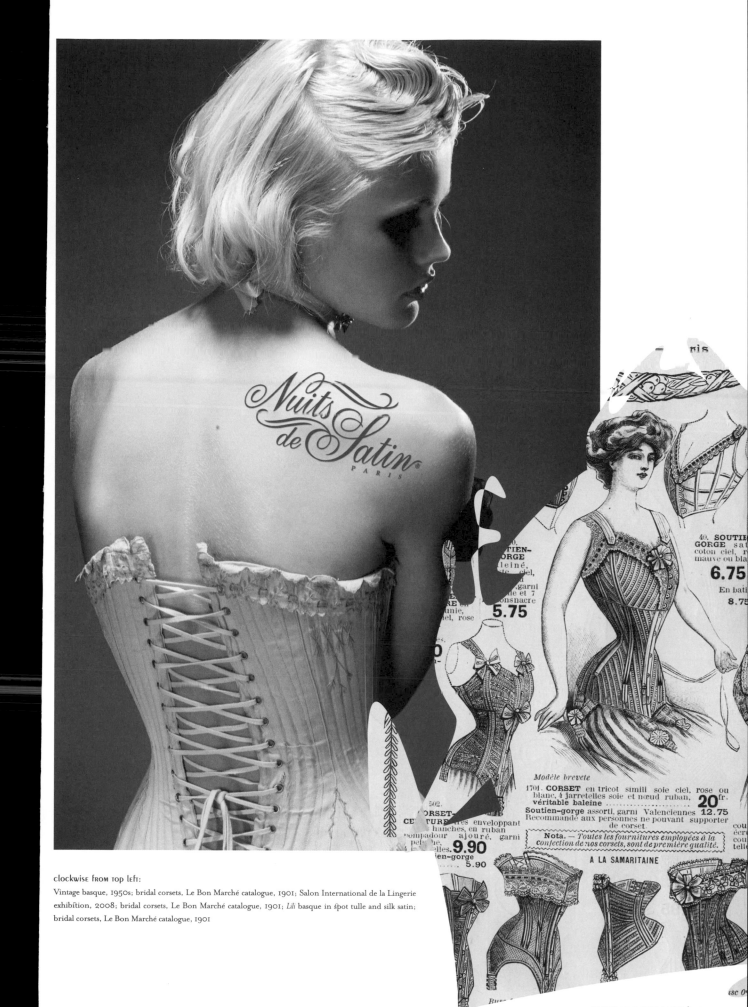

clockwise from top left:

Vintage basque, 1950s; bridal corsets, Le Bon Marché catalogue, 1901; Salon International de la Lingerie exhibition, 2008; bridal corsets, Le Bon Marché catalogue, 1901; *Lili* basque in spot tulle and silk satin; bridal corsets, Le Bon Marché catalogue, 1901

LEFT TO RIGHT:
Pin-up, Pleasure State White Label and *Liaison*, Pleasure State Couture, both Autumn/Winter 2008/09

PLEASURE STATE 〰

Pleasure State has brought fashion into lingerie, offering the rich fabrics and styling normally reserved for designer apparel. Kay Cohen is the brains behind Pleasure State, and it's her experience in understanding women's desire for both glamour and fit that has made the Sydney–based empire so successful.

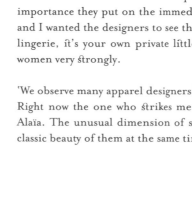

'I grew up on our family farm in New Zealand. I first fell in love with fashion when I was about twelve, pestering my mother to find me a dressmaker so I could have fashionable clothes. I studied Clothing and Textile Design at (what is now) Massey University in Wellington, New Zealand. Later I took an MBA, which allowed me to explore both the creative and the commercial aspects of being in business.

'My first 15 years were in fashion. Then followed a career in large corporate lingerie companies, first at Triumph International, then in New Zealand with the Bendon Group and Elle Macpherson Intimates.

'In 2003 I was employed in my third large company facing the same strategies I had implemented in the past two. I asked myself, "If this were my business, what would it look like"? From there I was able to create Pleasure State in 2004, and given some of my past experiences it was very clear what to do and what not to do. At its core, Pleasure State is about design. The product is everything and it always will be.

'I knew that this business could grow rapidly; it's not as if I were a young designer starting out. Finding the right partners has allowed Pleasure State to be international from the outset. Along with my business partner Justin Davis-Rice, we've grown Pleasure State into a brand of five labels sold in thirty-five countries.'

THE PLEASURE STATE WOMAN
〰

'She is us. She is me. I look around and it's for the women who are in my life, my work environment, in the world. The most important thing is that we love it as individuals and as a collective. The moment you start describing your customer or someone else you don't have a brand.'

THE INSPIRATIONS FOR THE DESIGNS
〰

'Research! I give the design team a briefing to look outside of their immediate environment. I really like this study to be about human beings. It's what's occurring in the world around us — something about a particular culture will arouse our interest. For example, we've just been to Japan to look at the importance they put on the immediate little things in life. It's immaculate, and I wanted the designers to see this and reference it back to lingerie. With lingerie, it's your own private little world and these tiny details appeal to women very strongly.

'We observe many apparel designers' work; Balenciaga was a recent favourite. Right now the one who strikes me as doing the most interesting things is Alaïa. The unusual dimension of some of the clothes and yet the absolute classic beauty of them at the same time is just the perfect marriage.'

FABRICS AND TRIMS

'Our fabrics and trims come from all over the world. We source most of our laces and silks in France. Many of our high-end fabrics also come from Italy, Belgium and Spain. We develop many of our components in China with our partner suppliers, as the technologies available to us to make superior bra cups and fabrics are at the cutting edge of technology.'

FAVOURITE FABRICS

'About the time I started the brand, a whole new range of very fine wovens with stretch became available. They are perfect for lingerie because they are not too stretchy; they have just the right amount of controlling, supportive stretch. In satin, for example, which can be in silk or a high-end polyester, it gives a perfectly flat, smooth finish and it will never snag like a knitted fabric. We can get a really crisp tailored look with them. Most of those fabrics come from France and Italy.'

FAVOURITE COLLECTIONS

'The first collection was the biggest challenge, as I had to make a clear statement about how Pleasure State was going to look. Core elements, such as the smooth-line tailoring, the wider bra straps and the Swarovski crystal detailing, have carried through all the following collections. This is important, as a brand must have a recognizable handwriting that it can own. Every season, I look at the final collection and I think this is the best yet … until we finalize the next one!'

FAVOURITE DESIGN

'Our bras! I am very proud of our superbly fitting and comfortable bra cups, which are seamless, smooth, flattering and exquisitely beautiful. In 2005 Pleasure State invented a graduated cup technology for a push-up bra that gives a great uplifting shape. It's almost the perfect formula for a bra. We use this cup in our fashion bras. It has become the world's best-selling shape for an everyday basic smooth bra.'

GLOBAL MARKET

'Our collections are released to the global market all at the same time. We find today that colour is an evolution and has little impact from the weather being hot or cold. We still refer to collections by their seasonal names, but for Pleasure State the influences are more likely to be around fashion seasons and events such as Christmas, Valentine's Day and Mother's Day.'

PHOTOGRAPHY AND STYLING

'All the creative thinking, art direction, model casting and styling around the photoshoots is decided internally between the design and marketing team. We are the ones building our image. We have been working with the same photographer, Steven Lyons, for the past four seasons. We take a fashionable and editorial approach to our photoshoots rather than focusing strictly on the product; we are showing the dream and the lifestyle that surrounds the Pleasure State woman.'

'All the creative thinking, art direction, model casting and styling around the photoshoots is decided internally between the design and marketing team. We are the ones building our image.'

clockwise from left:

Ole! Illustration; *Tango* illustration; White Label, Autumn/Winter 2008/09;
White Label moodboard Autumn/Winter 2008/09

TCN

T O ON COMELLA

TCN ❦

Totón Comella is the designer behind the Spanish label TCN. Starting out with swimwear, Totón has grown TCN from its roots in Barcelona into a well-known lingerie and loungewear label that blurs the boundaries between inner and outerwear and creates pieces that display a modern approach to lingerie dressing.

'I was born in the town of Arenys de Mar, close to Barcelona, in the 1960s. As a child, I first came into contact with the world of textiles through the family business. I remember summer holidays in Saint-Tropez, where we had a clothes shop and I would play and hide among the tailor's dummies, changing rooms and shelves. By the age of ten, I was already producing sketches of designs and patterns. At the time, I really wanted to be an artist, a painter and an interior designer, so I studied interior design and fine art.

'In 1984, by chance, I was given the opportunity to create a swimwear collection – in any fabric I chose, as long as the designs were very new and different. I picked cotton/Lycra jersey, a fabric that at the time was practically unknown. The collection was incredibly successful and I worked hard to promote it, travelling all around Spain to sell my designs.

'The huge number of orders forced me to reconsider my future and I launched the TCN label, at first based from an apartment in Barcelona. The swimwear line grew, and in 1991 I helped swimwear become a category in its own right at Barcelona's Gaudí catwalk shows, where I presented a collection every year.

'After ten years' success with swimwear, I ventured into the world of lingerie in 1995, with a line of corsetry, underwear and homewear. For the lingerie, I carried through the key features of comfort and simplicity that were so important to me in the swimwear.'

THE TCN APPROACH
❦

'My lingerie is based on a look that is natural, glamorous and sensual. The hallmarks of my early swimwear collections – comfort and simplicity – are still a constant in my garments. The comfort formula works effectively: top-quality fabrics, simple but original shapes and well-made garments.

'It's really important for me that my styles are recognizable year after year, regardless of what is in fashion. I always wanted TCN to be a trend-setting brand with fresh, fun colours and the latest fashion trends. I now present all my collections together – lingerie, swimwear, outerwear, childrenswear – every season at Madrid-Cibeles Fashion Week.'

THE TCN SECRET
❦

'The TCN secret is my firm belief in the three Cs:
Creation – the garment says look at me!
Caring about quality – the garment says touch me!
Comfort – the garment says try me!
The end result – the garment says take me with you!'

clockwise from top left:
Catwalk show, 2006; catwalk show, 2006;
Almirante store, Madrid; Paseo de Gracia
store, Barcelona

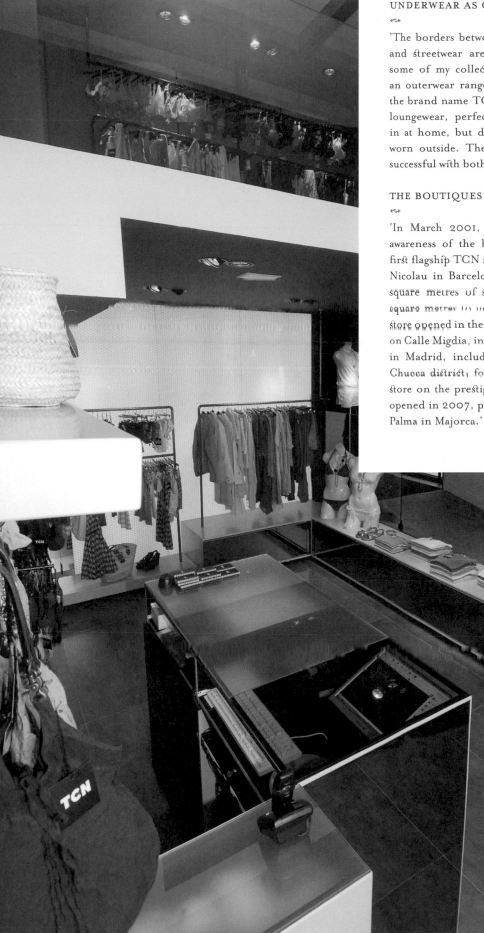

UNDERWEAR AS OUTERWEAR

❧

'The borders between day and night, sleepwear
and streetwear are practically non-existent in
some of my collections. In 2000, I launched
an outerwear range, two seasons a year, under
the brand name TCN-bis, which is comfortable
loungewear, perfect for sleeping and relaxing
in at home, but does not look out of place if
worn outside. The collection was immediately
successful with both buyers and press alike.'

THE BOUTIQUES

❧

'In March 2001, to create a greater overall
awareness of the brand and its products, the
first flagship TCN store opened on Calle Mestre
Nicolau in Barcelona. In addition to the 200
square metres of store space, I had over 300
square metres to use as a showroom. My second
store opened in the nearby Catalan city of Girona
on Calle Migdia, in 2002. I now have three stores
in Madrid, including one in the fashionable
Chueca district, four in Barcelona, including a
store on the prestigious Paseo de Gracia, which
opened in 2007, plus boutiques in Valencia and
Palma in Majorca.'

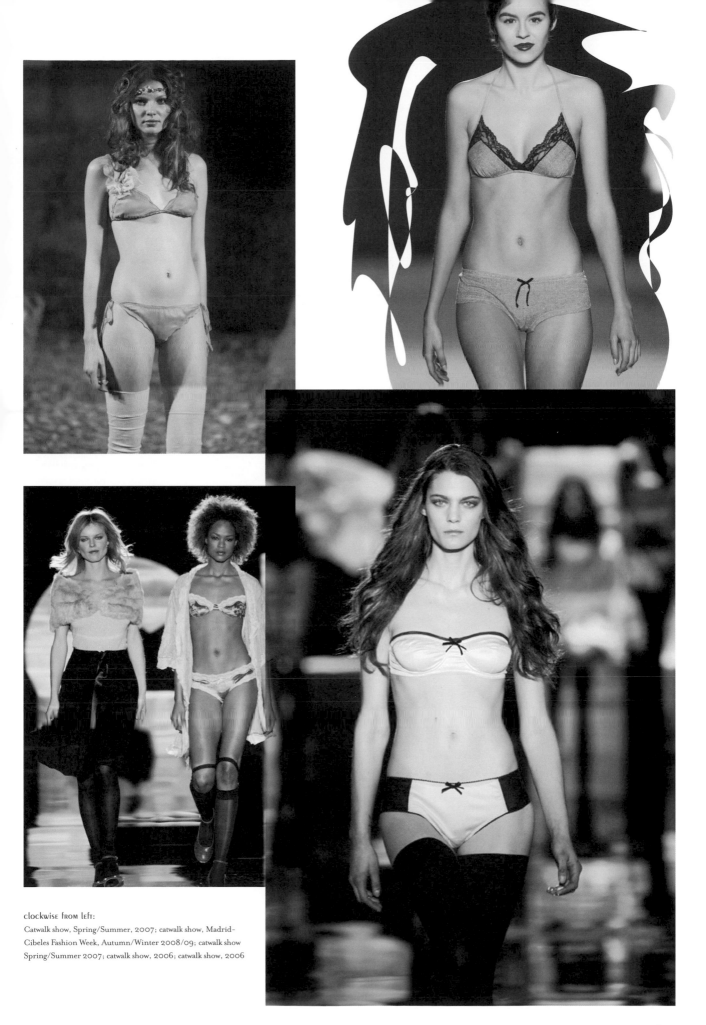

clockwise from left:
Catwalk show, Spring/Summer, 2007; catwalk show, Madrid-Cibeles Fashion Week, Autumn/Winter 2008/09; catwalk show Spring/Summer 2007; catwalk show, 2006; catwalk show, 2006

clockwise from top left:

Miss Tobacco, Spring/Summer 2009; influences, Spring/Summer 2009; *Miss Wild Pansy*, Spring/Summer 2009

Viola Sky 〜

Sonja Christensen and Dianna Wittig are the designers behind Viola Sky. Their lingerie has a soft feminine charm that fuses 1950s Parisian glamour with the fresh openness of their Danish heritage. Their cosy boutique in Copenhagen is proudly representative of a city famous for its stylish interiors.

'We were both born in Copenhagen and we always loved fashion and making our own clothes as teenagers, as we didn't have much money. We met in 1999 when we were both studying at the Hellerup Textile Academy just outside Copenhagen. We instantly fell in love with each other's creative skills and talents and realized that we would be a stronger combination if we worked together.

'The idea for Viola Sky started while we were at the academy, but it took a couple of years before we started working on the first collection in 2001. We used this time to save up the capital required for the project and to take various business courses. At first our collections were very small and we did fashion prêt-à-porter as well as lingerie. But the buyers always chose the lingerie, so we decided to do only lingerie.'

THE VIOLA SKY WOMAN
〜

'When we are creating our designs, it is always the Viola Sky woman who we have in mind. She is the ultimate feminine woman who is in us all.'

THE INSPIRATIONS FOR THE DESIGNS
〜

'We like the beauty of the 1950s Paris boudoir look, which is feminine, exquisite and also sexy, in a rather innocent way. We like the colours and the moods it inspires.

'Colours and colour combinations inspire us, and also silhouettes that enhance the female figure. We soak up inspiration on our travels to London and Paris. Sonja can be inspired in the garden and Dianna on the train to work — seeing a beautiful landscape in a split second as it passes by.

'Our lingerie has a Danish influence, as it's a bit more Scandinavian in style, more simple and with fewer frills than, for example, French lingerie.'

THE DESIGN PROCESS
〜

'Each collection starts with a gathering of ideas, sketches, cuttings from newspapers and magazines as well as a trip to either Interfilière or Première Vision fabric fair in Paris. We then narrow down our ideas and decide on the colours and colour combinations. After the sample fabrics arrive in the Viola Sky studio, the whole process of designing and fitting begins. Our fabrics come from Europe and our production is done in a factory in Eastern Europe with which we have a wonderful close relationship.'

PAST COLLECTIONS
〜

'We have a love of colour and shape that is apparent in all our collections. Each new collection is a favourite, so we can't choose between our children.

'As the designs develop, new ideas are born. But we are very proud of our high-waist panties, which are sexily cool and selling really well.'

THE BOUTIQUE

'Our flagship boutique in the centre of Copenhagen opened in 2005, because we thought it was important to create a physical Viola Sky universe and give our customers the experience of luxury and total femininity.

'The shop is like a pastel-coloured boudoir, where the lingerie hangs from cream-coloured satin-padded hangers. Some pieces appear served up on pretty cake plates inspired by French pâtisseries. Laidback jazz music plays softly.

'Besides carrying the complete Viola Sky collection, the store also sells a few other carefully selected lingerie brands, plus antique kimonos, accessories handpicked in Paris, a varied range of soaps and silk purses with humorous prints.'

CLOCKWISE FROM ABOVE:
Vintage French postcard inspiration; *Miss Wild Pansy*, Spring/Summer 2009; vintage French postcard inspiration; *Miss Bell* slip and knickers and design drawings, Spring/Summer 2009; the design process

clockwise from right page:
Miss Poppy and design drawings, Spring/Summer 2009; Autumn/Winter 2008/09; Copenhagen boutique; Autumn/Winter 2008/09

'We like the beauty of the 1950s Paris boudoir look, which is feminine, exquisite and also sexy, in a rather innocent way. We like the colours and the moods it inspires.'

clockwise from bottom left:
Brand exhibition, Autumn/Winter
2007; brand exhibition, Autumn/
Winter 2007; inspired by clusters
of large chrysanthemum flowers,
this design is very Japanese in style
and expresses a strong WACOAL DIA
handwriting, Autumn/Winter 2007

WACOAL DIA ❧

*WACOAL DIA sits at the pinnacle of the luxury lingerie market in Japan. Designed for Wacoal by Atsuko Kamio,
the label's essence comes from a blending of aesthetic traditions from Japan and France to create special pieces
that subtly redefine a very Japanese sense of beauty.*

WACOAL DIA is the ultra-luxury label from the Wacoal Corporation, which is
a major player in the global lingerie market today and Japan's best-known
brand. In 2004, the label was launched with its own boutique in Tokyo's
upmarket Ginza district. The highly regarded designer Atsuko Kamio was
invited to be the 'total creator' of WACOAL DIA, meaning that she oversees all
aspects of the design of the collection.

Atsuko Kamio divides her time between Kyoto and her apartment in Saint-
Germain-des-Prés on Paris's fashionable Left Bank. 'I grew up in Saitama
near Tokyo. My mother was a fashion designer, which was a rare profession in
1950s Japan. I could sew when I was five and I made a jacket when I was nine
years old! My family was very rich in artistic sense and our home was full of
European influences such as fashion books, Western paintings, music, films
and beautiful clothes, as well as gorgeous Japanese kimonos.

'My mother would ask my opinion on aspects of fashion and design, so I was
already familiar with fashion before I went to study at the Sugino Gakuen
Dressmaker Gakuin design school in Tokyo. At the school I learned craft
skills, how to design and all about the fashion world, including European
haute couture and American-style apparel.

'We create contemporary exhibitions to explain the concept of the collection
to buyers, the press and VIP customers. I start by talking through the story
behind the collection to the set designer and then the exhibition is created.'

THE WACOAL DIA WOMAN
❧

'WACOAL DIA is designed for women with a sophisticated aesthetic sense. I
hope that a woman who wears our lingerie will respond to a very Japanese
concept of beauty. I want to give Japanese women confidence, highlighting
their beautiful features — velvety skin, flawless colouring and delicate figure.
When you wear our brand, you will feel elegant, luxurious and sexy from the
inside out.'

THE JAPANESE DESIGN ELEMENT
❧

'All the collections have a very Japanese feeling to them. The brand's concept
of cross-culture mixes together Japanese and European cultural ideas,
as well as crossing haute couture with prêt-à-porter, classic with modern,
technology with function and underwear with outerwear. Something totally
new is created when more than two ideas mingle and respond to each other.'

INSPIRATIONS FOR THE DESIGNS
❧

'I'm inspired by everything: nature, landscapes, antiques. I love historical
costume, accessories and drawings from the seventeenth to the nineteenth
centuries; I find this period the most beautiful. I especially love European

かがやける小袖の美

dress from the eighteenth and nineteenth centuries. From Japan I'm inspired by seventeenth to nineteenth century applied arts, kimono designs and paintings, especially Rimpa painting, from artists such as Ogata Kyrin.'

THE DESIGN PROCESS

'I start with colours, laces, fabrics and motifs. I think about all these aspects while I'm putting together the story for the collection. I look after all the stages in the design process, not just the concept. I draw the silhouettes and sketch out the lace and embroidery designs, as well as creating the first patterns.

'All the embroidery and lace patterns are based on traditional motifs taken from nature or classic textiles. Our exclusive fabrics, laces and embroideries come from Europe or Japan and all the garments are made in WACOAL's own factories in Japan.'

FAVOURITE DESIGNS

'WACOAL DIA features luxury Leavers lace, delicate tulle and original embroideries and laces. The silhouettes are very imaginative, with bras as light and delicate as a feather, ultra-feminine petticoats like a ballerina's tutu, laced tops reminiscent of corsets, and silk jacquards from Lyon, France, that give a heavy noble effect to more outerwear pieces.'

THE BOUTIQUES

'The lingerie is very delicate, luxurious, elegant and very feminine, while the interior of the boutique is modern, hard, monotone in colour and very masculine. The boutique doesn't need to have a boudoir-style interior because the lingerie is sufficiently sexy itself.

'After the first store in Ginza in 2004, a second boutique opened in 2007 in Tokyo Midtown, in the highly fashionable Roppongi area. WACOAL DIA lingerie is also available in three boutiques set within the most upmarket Japanese department stores in Tokyo: Isetan in Shinjuku and Seibu in Shibuya and Ikebukuro. There is also a boutique within Sogo department store in Yokohama.'

clockwise from bottom left:
Embroidery represents the Winter 2008 theme, with eight different types of glittering snow crystals dancing across a fine tulle, Autumn/Winter 2008; Japanese inspiration for the collections; design sketches; embroidery representing the Winter 2008 theme; brand exhibition, Autumn/Winter 2008

Embroidery onto tulle depicting water ripples frozen into the form of a flower, Autumn/Winter 2008; a delicate Chantilly lace is used for the cross-over *echarpe*, which is very WACOAL DIA in style; the tulle petticoat is the brand's signature piece and appears every season in different colours and designs – the piece shown is from Autumn/Winter 2007; design sketches; embroidery sketches; design sketches

GLOSSARY OF LINGERIE TERMS ⟿

BABYDOLL: short, loose-fitting nightdress, styled into an A-line silhouette or empire-line with bust seaming. Popularized in the 1950s, often made in sheer chiffon, tulle or nylon tricot. Styling is ultra-feminine, with bows, frills and ribbons. Usually worn with a small brief, such as a string.

BALCONY BRA: underwired bra with low-cut square-shaped neckline. The straps are placed wide, further away from the neck than on a standard bra, often attached to the outer edge of the wiring.

BALLET-WRAP: small top, with short or long sleeves, whose front sections cross over forming a V-neckline, with long ties that knot at the waist.

BANDEAU BRA: strapless bra, often non-wired and in a simple, sporty design.

BASQUE: lightly figure-shaping style of corset with suspender straps, often with boning but no lacing.

BATISTE: lightweight opaque plain-weave cotton fabric, popularized for lingerie in the Victorian and Edwardian periods.

BED JACKET: short jacket or cape originating from the eighteenth century. It finishes above the waist, and is worn in bed over nightclothes.

BIAS: the diagonal of a woven fabric, 45 degrees to a fabric's warp and weft threads. Garments made from woven fabrics cut close to the body, such as slips, are traditionally cut on the bias.

BIKINI BRIEF: hipster brief popularized in the 1970s.

BOBBINET: the most popular pattern of tulle that creates a hexagonal design.

BONING: used to support a corset, the bones were traditionally made from whalebone and, later, steel. Steel boning comes in either flat or spiral form. Today mass-produced corsetry uses nylon boning.

BODY: close-fitting garment covering the torso and fastening between the legs. It can be worn as underwear or the top part as outerwear. Styling ranges from strappy, low to high necklines, short or long sleeves, underwired cups, string or short leglines. They are usually made in stretch lace or tulle and stretch jerseys.

BODY STOCKING: a seamless body that reaches down to the ankles, often worn by dancers.

BOXER SHORTS: originally a men's underwear item; loose-fitting underwear shorts, traditionally in fine woven cotton.

BOY SHORT: US term for a brief styled as a skimpy version of a man's short, often cut low on the hips.

BRA: from the French term *brassière*, meaning bodice. Developed in the early twentieth century, the bra is designed to support and shape the breasts. Composed of two cups, with or without wiring, the bra is usually held up by shoulder-straps and is most often fastened at the back by hooks and eyes.

BRA PAD: small cushion of foam covered with fabric that fits into the cup of the bra to give the bust an uplifted silhouette. These are sometimes removable.

BRA WIRE: a thin semi-circular strip of metal with a nylon coating at both ends that fits inside the bra casing running around the lower edge of the bra cup. Wires come in different sizes and shapes to give different cup silhouettes.

BRIEF: UK term for all styles of underwear covering the genital area, running from the waist or hips with two openings for the legs.

BRODERIE ANGLAISE: traditional whitework embroidery on fine white cotton, linen or muslin, characterized by designs made up of small holes or eyelets created in buttonhole stitch.

BUSTIER: traditionally, a strapless piece of corsetry that is either boned and/or underwired and finishes at or above the waist. Today its meaning has expanded to include corsetry pieces with shoulder straps.

CAMIKNICKER: *see* Short all-in-one.

CAMISOLE: small top, usually with fine straps, worn slightly loose-fitting under outerwear, smoothing out the outline of the bra. Also worn today as a decorative outerwear top.

CHANTILLY LACE: originally made in the town of Chantilly, France, this lace is characterized by a fine tulle ground and delicate flowers and scrolls, and the pattern is often outlined with heavy silk thread.

CHEMISE: US term for underwear or nightwear slip-dress.

CHIFFON: plain-weave sheer fabric, usually in silk or polyester.

CORSELETTE: a garment that combines bra and girdle, popular from the 1920s onwards and most popular in the 1950s. Usually designed with integral underwired bra and suspender straps.

CORSET: classic undergarment of rigid fabric, most often boned and adjusted by means of laces, designed to mould the body from the bust to the hip. Designs vary from era to era, with some corsets starting below the bust or ending at the waist. Often designed with suspender straps to hold up stockings.

CORSET COVER: piece of lingerie worn over the corset in the Victorian and Edwardian periods to protect expensive outwear from being damaged by the rigid parts of the corset.

CORSETRY: a term that applies to all underwear that supports, such as the bra, corset and waspie.

CRÊPE DE CHINE: lightweight woven fabric with a slight 'spring', usually in silk or polyester and cut on the bias, popularized for use in lingerie in the 1920s and 1930s.

CRINOLINE: circular skirt-shaped cage of whalebone or metal wire that developed in the mid-nineteenth century to support skirts, taking over from the use of stiff horsehair or 'crin' woven with cotton/linen. The crinoline supported the voluminous full skirts, allowing them to balloon out.

CROCHET LACE: chunky cotton lace traditionally made by hand, today mostly produced by machine.

CUP: a pocket of a bra that supports the breast and gives the bust a beautiful shape.

CYCLING SHORT: a short ending mid-thigh, worn for sport, generally made in nylon/elastane.

DRESSING GOWN: UK term for coat-style garment worn around the house over underwear or nightwear. Known as a robe in the USA.

ELASTANE (ee also SPANDEX): a synthetic fibre known for its elasticity. Invented by DuPont in 1959, it revolutionized close-fitting lingerie, allowing garments to support and shape the body while stretching to fit, thereby eliminating the need for fastenings. The most well-known tradename is Lycra from Invista (formally part of DuPont). Known as spandex in the USA.

EMBROIDERY: decoration of a fabric with ornamental motifs created by yarns and tiny three-dimensional trim details.

FRENCH KNICKER: classic loose-fitting brief, developed in the 1920s and 1930s, often in a luxurious woven fabric cut on the bias.

FULL SLIP: a lightweight sleeveless lingerie piece, usually with thin straps, worn under a dress or skirt and coming in several lengths.

FULLY-FASHIONED STOCKINGS: made on traditional machinery that knits the stocking as a flat item, which is then sewn up the back to create a back seam. These stockings can also have distinctive heel designs and both seam and heel can be in a contrasting colour.

GARTER: ribbon or strip of elastic that serves to keep the stocking on the thigh.

GIRDLE: support underwear piece developed in the first half of the twentieth century to replace the corset, designed to shape the waist and the hips and hold in the stomach. Popularized in the second half of the twentieth century by the use of elastane fibres. Often given suspender straps to allow stockings to be attached. Today the girdle is often shortened into a style of suspender belt, covering from the hip to the thigh.

G-STRING: a brief consisting of a front panel only and elastic running around the hips and between the legs. Synonymous with string and thong.

GUÊPIÈRE: French term for waspie, from the French guêpe, for wasp.

GUIPURE: traditionally, a type of heavy lace with no ground net. Today it is created on an embroidery machine, the yarns stitched onto a net that is then chemically dissolved away.

HALF-SLIP: lightweight skirt worn under an outerwear skirt, coming in several lengths. Also known as a waist-slip.

HOLD-UP STOCKINGS: stockings that are kept in place with the help of a band of elastic or silicone placed at the top part of the stocking; often decorated with lace.

HOOKS AND EYES: small metal fastenings that allow two pieces of a garment to attach together.

HOUSECOAT: style of lightweight coat of various lengths worn by women around the house in the 1950s. Today used in a kitsch or retro fashion.

KIMONO: styled from the traditional Japanese kimono, a T-shaped robe in woven cotton or silk with wide sleeves and often printed with large patterns.

KNEE-HIGHS: circular-knit socks that finish below the knee, mostly worn under trousers.

KNICKERS: classic UK term for all styles of brief, similar to panties in the USA.

GLOSSARY CONTINUED ⤳

LACE: openwork textile created from yarn in decorative patterns, often floral. Traditionally made by hand, today made by machine.

LACING: system to tighten a corset; most corsets are back-laced.

LEAVERS LACE: the first machine-made lace, developed in the nineteenth century. It is now the most expensive form of machine-made lace, as Leavers machines are capable of the finest quality and the most intricate designs, and because these machines are no longer built, thus limiting production.

LEGGINGS: originally a man's underwear garment made from jersey, covering the bottom half of the body, in different leg-lengths. Today worn more often by women (¾-length or to the ankle) in thermal fabrics for warmth, and also as a fashionable outerwear item knitted from thick opaque yarns.

LYCRA: well-known brand name of elastane stretch fibre.

MICROFIBRE: fabric made from synthetic fibres that measure less than one denier. The most common types of microfibres are made from polyesters, polyamides (nylon), or a blend of polyester and polyamide. Today microfibre is the most popular fabric used for functional, everyday bras and briefs.

MOULDED BRA: bra with seamless moulded cups; either the whole cup or just the foam padding is shaped by heat-moulding technology to form a sized cup.

MOUSSELINE: French term for muslin. A lightweight fabric, usually in cotton or silk.

MULTIWAY BRA: bra with straps that can be adapted to make the bra strapless, with a halter neckline or with cross-over straps at the back (racer-back).

NEGLIGEE: from the French *négligée* meaning neglected, originating from eighteenth-century France as a form of nightgown to be worn around the house. From the 1950s onwards the term has come to mean a lightweight robe or gown worn over a nightdress, often in a sheer fabric, such as chiffon.

NIGHTDRESS: garment worn for sleeping in, resembling a dress and coming in different lengths.

NIGHTSHIRT: loose-fitting long shirt worn for sleeping in, unisex, and often in brushed cottons for warmth in winter.

NUISETTE: French term for babydoll.

PEIGNOIR: from the French *peigner*, to comb the hair. A long, lightweight coat worn in the home, originally worn at the toilette whilst combing long hair. Today synonymous with the negligee.

PETTICOAT: underwear skirt with a fitted waist. Popularized in the 1950s with tiered, ruffled stiffened petticoats in fabrics such as nylon, chiffon, taffeta and tulle. Today revived as a fashion item, often in bright colours. Also used as a term for a full slip.

PINTUCKS: decorative narrow parallel tucks often used on lingerie.

PLUNGE BRA: bra with a low V-shaped neckline, often padded to give the bust an uplifted silhouette.

POLYAMIDE: generic term for synthetic polymers, the most well known being nylon, with brands such as Tactel and Meryl.

POLYESTER: synthetic polymer fibre, popularized in the 1970s. It is characterized by being quick-drying, hard-wearing and taking bright colours and prints well. Retro 1970s polyester nightwear has become a source of inspiration for today's designers.

PUSH-UP BRA: bra with padding to give the bust an uplifted silhouette, with a low V-shaped neckline.

PYJAMAS: from an Indian term for trousers, pyjamas were popularized in the late nineteenth century as loungewear by British colonials bringing the custom back from Asia. Later developed into the nightwear jacket and trousers for men and today also worn by women.

RACER-BACK: the arrangement of bra straps that run across the shoulders and cross over at the centre back, leaving the shoulders bare. Often used in sports bras or under sleeveless tops.

ROBE: US term for coat-style garment worn around the house over underwear or nightwear. Known as a dressing gown in the UK.

SECOND-SKIN LINGERIE: modern term meaning bra, brief and camisoles that mould the body and are often seamless.

SHAPEWEAR: modern term to describe lingerie pieces that offer extra support, especially control knickers.

SHORT ALL-IN-ONE: also called a camiknicker, originally a light underwear piece popularized in the 1920s, composed of a top with fine straps joined to a loose-fitting short, often fastening between the legs. Today styled less fussily and made from modern fashion fabrics. Also known as a teddy.

SHORTIE/SHORTY: short-style brief, designed to be skimpier than a classic short, often with feminine detailing.

SHOULDER STRAP: narrow band, usually adjustable and elastic with stretch, that passes over the shoulder and joins the back and the front of a bra.

SPANDEX (see also ELASTANE): a synthetic fibre known for its elasticity. Invented by DuPont in 1959, it revolutionized close-fitting lingerie, allowing garments to support and shape the body while stretching to fit, thereby eliminating the need for fastenings. The most well-known tradename is Lycra from Invista (formally part of DuPont). Known as elastane outside the USA.

SPORTS BRA: bra used for sports, offering extra comfort and support to counter the extra movement of the body.

STOCKINGS: pieces of clothing that cover the foot and the leg to beyond the knee. Worn with a suspender belt or garters. Traditionally made by hand in cotton or silk, today made by machine.

STRAPLESS BRA: bra with no shoulder straps, often padded, popularized in the 1950s. Today kept in place by a band of silicone elastic running around top edge of the underband of the bra.

STRING: see G-string.

STRING-BACK BODY: body with a G-string back.

SUSPENDER BELT: belt worn around the waist, designed with suspender straps used to attach stockings. Known in the US as a garter belt.

SUSPENDER KNICKER: brief with suspender straps, often detachable.

SUSPENDER STRAP: a strip of elastic attached at the base of a corset, girdle or suspender belt ending with a clasp that fastens to the top hem of a stocking, keeping the stocking in place.

T-SHIRT BRA: bra with seamless moulded cups, popularized in the USA as the ideal bra to wear under jersey and close-fitting tops and dresses.

TANGA: skimpy style of brief where front and back panels are held together by elastic or ribbon at the sides.

TEDDY: see Short all-in-one.

THONG: see G-string.

TIGHTS: a combination of stockings with an integral brief created on a circular knitting machine that gives the brief and leg shape. Varying the yarn can create ultra-sheer tights through to opaque, chunky versions.

TRIANGLE BRA: non-wired bra popularized in the 1960s and 1970s, with a simple elastic band around the torso and skimpy triangle-shaped cups over the breasts.

TULLE: a lightweight net traditionally made in the French town of Tulle. It is most commonly made from nylon but can be also produced from silk or cotton blends.

UNDERBAND: part of the bra that runs around the torso and into which the cups are sewn.

UNDERWIRING: semi-circle of metal or plastic placed around the base of the two cups of a bra, giving a better support to the breast as well as separating the breasts.

VEST: knitted underwear top, sleeveless or with fine straps, traditionally created on a circular knitting machine.

VISCOSE: cellulose fibre made from wood, often used as a jersey fabric for lingerie, characterized by a soft drape and its high-lustre quality.

WAIST-SLIP: lightweight skirt, worn under an outerwear skirt, often coming in several lengths. Also known as a half-slip.

WASPIE: short corset circling the waist, most often fastened by laces or hooks and eyes.

WHITEWORK: style of embroidery in which white fabric is stitched with white threads, popularized during the Victorian and Edwardian periods.

WING: the side part of the underband of the bra, running from the outer edge of the cups around to the centre back.

CONTRIBUTOR CONTACTS ᜆ

A.F. VANDEVORST
Indiëstraat 8
2000 Antwerp, Belgium
+32 3 201 30 90
info@afvandevorst.be
www.afvandevorst.be

ANDRES SARDA
Madrid Boutiques:
Don Ramón de la Cruz, 14
28001 Madrid
+34 915 78 15 45
Marbella boutique:
Av. Ricardo Soriano, 12
29601 Marbella
andressarda@eurocorset.com
www.andressarda.com

BIEN FÉE POUR TOI
+33 1 42 64 32 83
contact@bienfeepourtoi.com
www.bienfeepourtoi.com

CAROL MALONY
17383 Sunset Blvd. Suite A101
Pacific Palisades, CA 90272, USA
+1 310 230 8072
cmlingerie@aol.com
www.carolmalony.com

CHANTAL THOMASS
Paris Boutique:
211, rue Saint Honoré
75001 Paris, France
+33 1 42 60 40 56
www.chantalthomass.fr

CLAIRE PETTIBONE
Claire Pettibone boutique:
236 South Robertson Blvd.
Beverly Hills, CA 90016, USA
+1 310 360 6268
customerservice@clairepettibone.com
www.clairepettibone.com

ELISE ANDEREGG
13 rue Versigny
75018 Paris, France
+ 33 663 593 777
eliseanderegg@aol.com
www.eliseanderegg.com

ELISE AUCOUTURIER
17 rue du Buhat
60300 Apremont, France
+33 3 44 54 76 47
contact@eliseaucouturier.com
www.eliseaucouturier.com

EVA RACHLINE
Paris boutique:
33 rue de Grenelle
75007 Paris, France
+33 1 45 48 05 99
boutique: boutique@evarachline.com
general: contact@evarachline.com
www.evarachline.com

FIFI CHACHNIL
Paris boutiques:
231 rue Saint Honoré 75001 Paris
+33 1 42 61 21 83
68 rue Jean-Jacques Rousseau 75001 Paris
+33 1 42 21 19 93
contact@fifichachnil.com
www.fifichachnil.com

FISHBELLY
Sophienstrasse 7
10178 Berlin, Germany
+49 30 280 451 80
mail@fishbelly.de
www.fishbelly.de

FLEUR OF ENGLAND
The Studio
103 Lower Redland Road,
Redland, Bristol BS6 6SW, England
+44 117 970 6701
info@fleurofengland.com
www.fleurofengland.com

GÂTEZ-MOI
Flora Ebisu #102,
2-15-5 Ebisu Minami, Shibuya-ku,
Tokyo 150-0022, Japan
+81 3 5724 4486
info@gatez-moi.com
www.gatez-moi.com

GENTRY DE PARIS
gentry@gentrydeparis.com
www.gentrydeparis.com
www.gentrydeparis
    burlesquerevue.com

GUIA LA BRUNA
I.G.E.A.T. SRL
Corso Verona 30
10153 Turin, Italy
+39 011 28 48 24
info@guialab.com
www.guialabruna.com

JEAN YU
New York atelier and boutique:
37 Crosby street
New York, NY 10013, USA
+1 212 226 0067
info@jeanyu.com
www.jeanyu.com

KYUIS
M.Y.Daikanyama,
3-1 Sarugakuchou
Shibuya-ku, Tokyo 150-0033, Japan
+81 3 3770 6339
kyuiskyuiskyuis@gmail.com

THE LAKE & STARS
458 11th st #2
Brooklyn, NY 11215, USA
+1 917 974 7374
info@thelakeandstars.com
www.thelakeandstars.com

LALA ROSE

SVA SARL
BKENNAYA
PÈRE YAACOUB STREET
NEEMTALLAH NADER BUILDING,
GROUND FLR
BEIRUT, LEBANON
+961 4 714818
+961 4 714819
LALAROSELB@YAHOO.FR
WWW.LALAROSE.COM

LEE KLABIN

78 KINGSLAND ROAD, FIRST FLOOR,
LONDON E2 8DP, ENGLAND
+44 207 619 1111
INFO@LEEKLABIN.COM
WWW.LEEKLABIN.COM

LOUISE FEUILLÈRE

PARIS ATELIER AND BOUTIQUE:
102 RUE DES DAMES
75017 PARIS, FRANCE
+33 1 42 93 17 76
LF@LOUISEFEUILLERE.COM
WWW.LOUISEFEUILLERE.COM

MADE BY NIKI

SYMINGTON HOUSE
14 SCHOOL LANE, MARKET HARBOROUGH
LEICESTERSHIRE LE16 9DJ, ENGLAND
+44 1858 432 141
INFO@MADEBYNIKI.CO.UK
WWW.MADEBYNIKI.CO.UK

MARLIES DEKKERS

+31 10 476 04 14
INFO@MARLIESDEKKERS.COM
WWW.MARLIESDEKKERS.COM

MISS LALA PRESENTS

COVENT GARDEN BOUTIQUE:
MISS LALA'S BOUDOIR
18 MONMOUTH STREET,
LONDON WC2H 9HB, ENGLAND
INFO@MISSLALAPRESENTS.COM
WWW.MISSLALAPRESENTS.COM

N DE SAMIM

9559 CEDARBROOK DRIVE
BEVERLY HILLS
CA 90210, USA
+1 310869 2570
NONASAMIMI@AOL.COM
WWW.NDESAMIM.COM

NUITS DE SATIN PARIS

PARIS SHOWROOM AND BOUTIQUE:
5 RUE JEAN BOLOGNE
75016 PARIS, FRANCE
+33 1 45 27 27 45
CONTACT@NUITSDESATIN.COM
WWW.NUITSDESATIN.COM

PLEASURE STATE

LEVEL 1 194 OXFORD STREET,
PADDINGTON NSW, AUSTRALIA
+612 9004 8077
INFO@PLEASURESTATE.COM
WWW.PLEASURESTATE.COM

TCN

NOESO SA (TCN)
RIAL BELLSOLELL, 30
08358 ARENYS DE MUNT
BARCELONA, SPAIN
+34 93 795 11 14
COMERCIAL@TCN.ES
KIM@TCN.ES
WWW.TCN.ES

VIOLA SKY

COPENHAGEN BOUTIQUE:
HYSKENSTRÆDE 16
1297 COPENHAGEN, DENMARK
VIOLASKY@VIOLASKY.DK
WWW.VIOLASKY.DK

WACOAL DIA

GINZA NAMIKI-DORI BOUTIQUE:
7-6-16 GINZA CYUO-KU TOKYO
104-0061, JAPAN
+81 3 5537 0850
WWW.WACOALDIA.COM

PICTURE CREDITS ↬

ACKNOWLEDGEMENTS

This book is the product of goodwill. It could not have been written without the help of a great many people working to design, produce and market the best of contemporary lingerie: designers, models and photographers and press representatives. To all of you, I offer my heart-felt thanks.

In particular, I wish to thank Lindsey Dupler for introducing me to Laurence King, and to commissioning editor Helen Evans who has made the whole project possible.

Lingerie and beauty journalist Yoshie Kawahara working in Tokyo gave me enormous help with the Japanese section. Thank you Yoshie.

And thank you to designer Charlotte Heal for a most original and memorable layout.

Last and by no means least, I should like to thank Barry Fantoni, my partner, for his constant support and encouragement.